UNNA DIARY

Peter Bialobrzeski

April 11 – April 16, 2021

Hartmann books

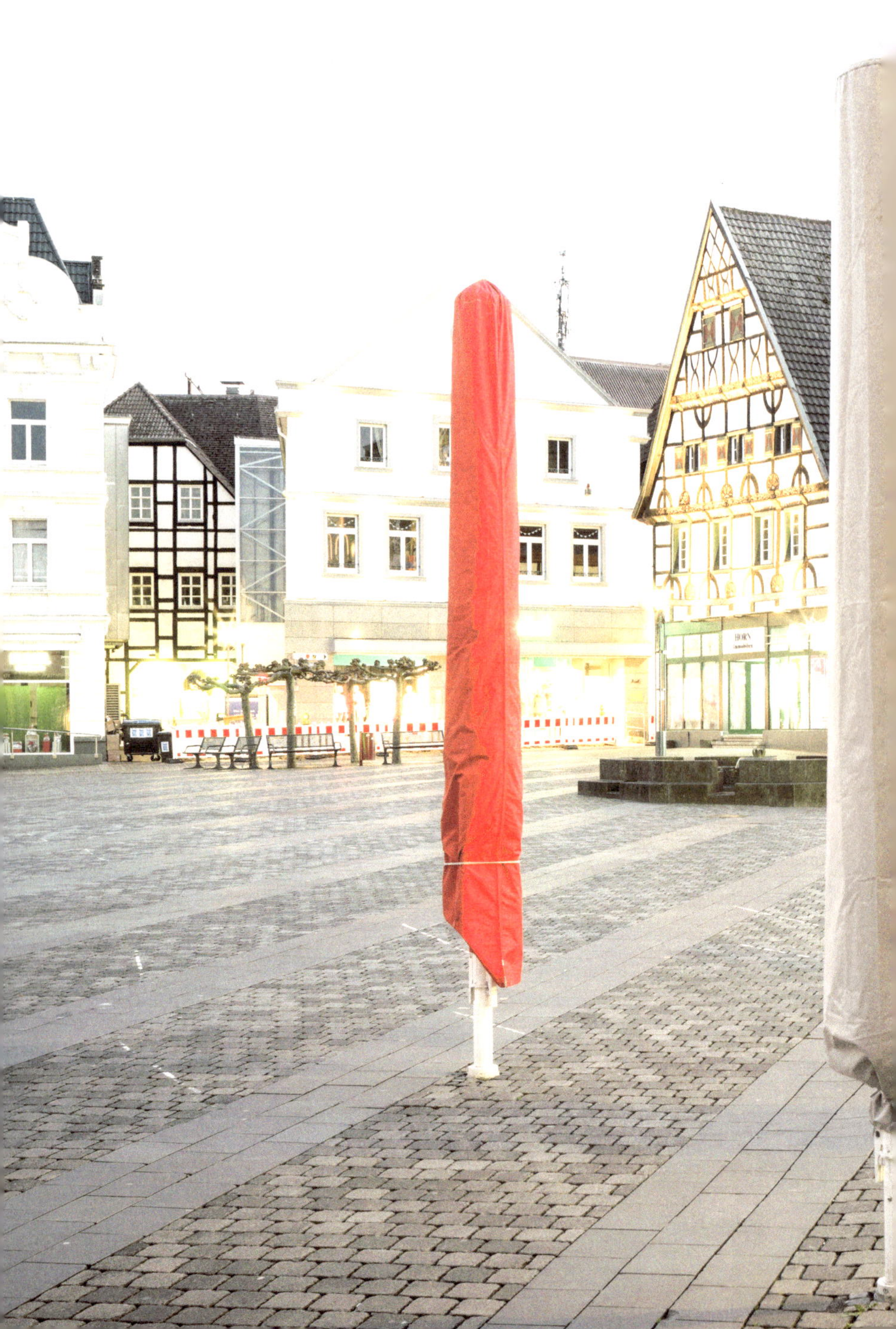

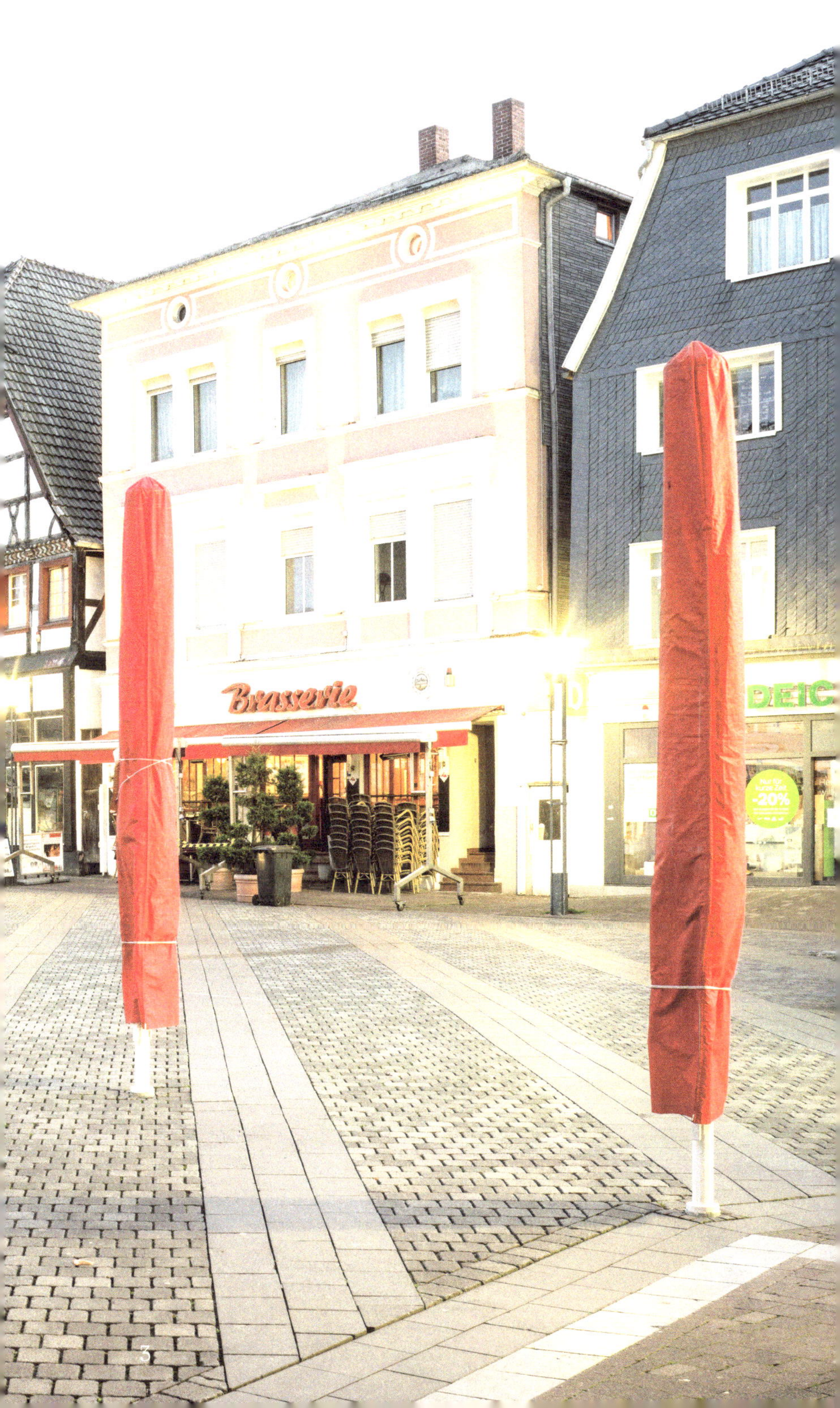
Brasserie
DEIC
-20%

UNNA DIARY

Peter Bialobrzeski

→ April 11, 2021 On a Sunday morning everyone walking in the main shopping street is supposed to wear a face mask, no matter whether there are other humans around. Juridical measures are holding a tight grip over the city. To me it does not make sense; my breath steams up my glasses as I try to photograph a city painted gray by the grim April rain. After my morning shoot, I meet Wolfgang Patzkowsky, a local who is a walking history book on the city's past. We take a stroll through the centuries, visiting the cellar of the local brewery as well as stopping for coffee in the studio of a lovely artist couple whose premises consist of a collection of homemade objects whose artistic value is hard to define but speak of a love for the eclectic. → April 12, 2021 The arts play a veritable part in the city. Most popular is a sculpture by one Josef Baron depicting a figure trying to pull a donkey, which for reasons unknown to most locals became the mascot of the city. Graffiti of a stylized version of the artifact can be found all over town. Rumors claim that the stubborn animal epitomizes the Westphalian mentality. The local paper claims that one of these stubborn inhabitants robbed a petrol station of some petty cash by presenting a *butcher's knife* to the girl at the counter. Furthermore, the local paper offers some in-depth reportage of locals getting vaccinated with the infamous AstraZeneca serum. → April 13, 2021 Antigen COVID tests are free and readily available at the local pharmacy around the corner. Results are supposed to be sent to the delinquent by email within a quarter of an hour. In spite of that a small crowd of locals queue in front of the venue in order to receive their statement as a printed matter. Fighting the pandemic digitally is not the number one priority for my fellow countrymates, I suppose. → April 14, 2021 When I start my morning walk at 6:30 I am accompanied from day one by a noisy motorized sweeper. The vanguard dressed in orange with a hoodie underneath is operating a leaf blower. One of his guilty pleasures is to blow a small white plastic bag aimlessly through the pedestrian zone. I can't help being reminded of the film *American Beauty*—without the beauty but with a lot of noise. When I ask him about the reasoning for his activity he explains to me in his nice local accent that his job is to stir up the filth, that the sweeper can do the rest. → April 15, 2021 I am made aware of an event in the city that I must have missed. Apparently fifteen people, I learn from the local paper, have held a demonstration against the *corona lockdown*. According to a spokesperson of that very group, a well-known right-wing activist, the gathering had attracted "considerable attention" within the city walls of Unna. → April 16, 2021 I receive a academic paper that puts the donkey issue into perspective: apparently in the nineteenth century a lot of the gray mules lived within the medieval city walls. The citizens of Unna were nicknamed *Unna donkeys*, no insult intended.

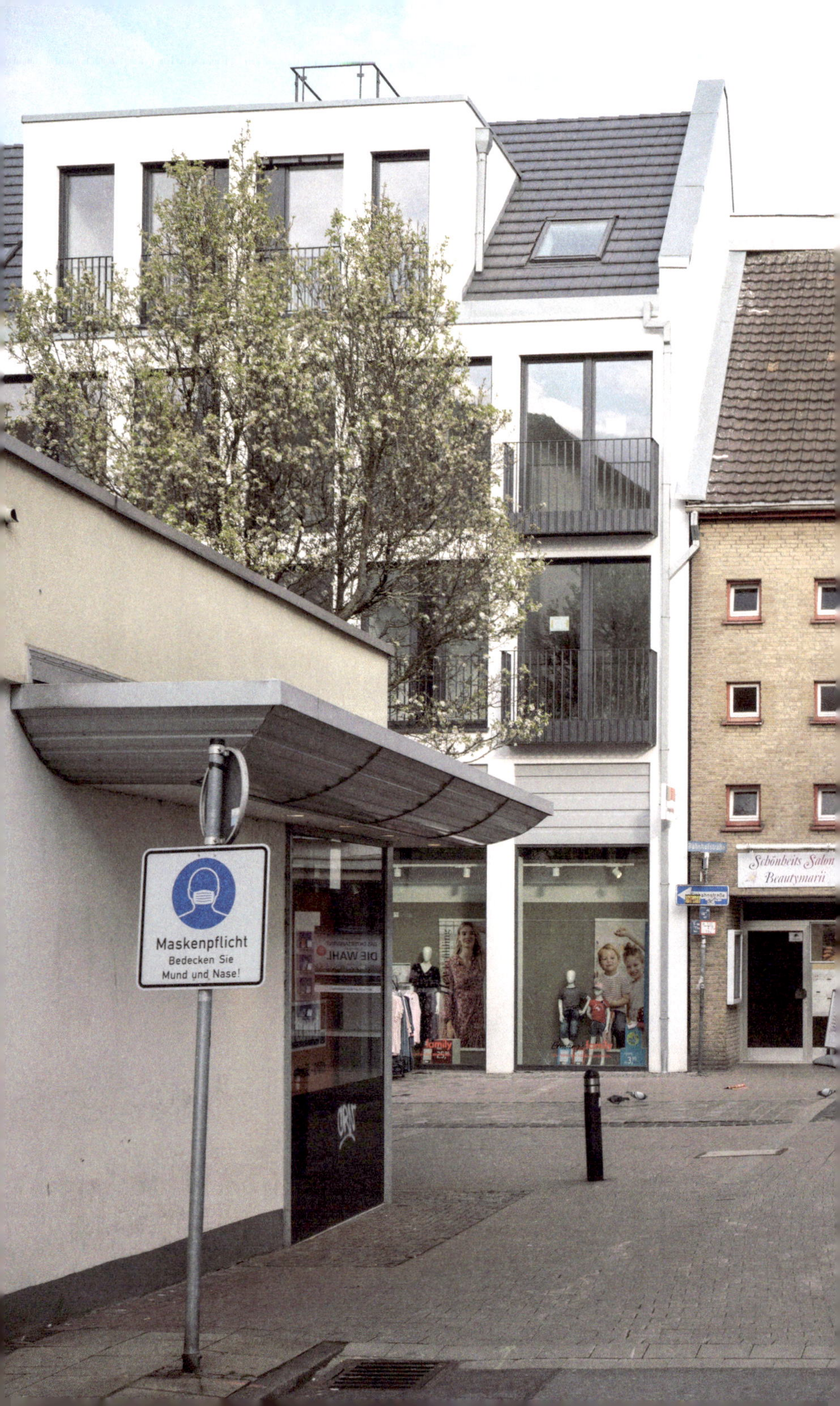
Maskenpflicht
Bedecken Sie
Mund und Nase!

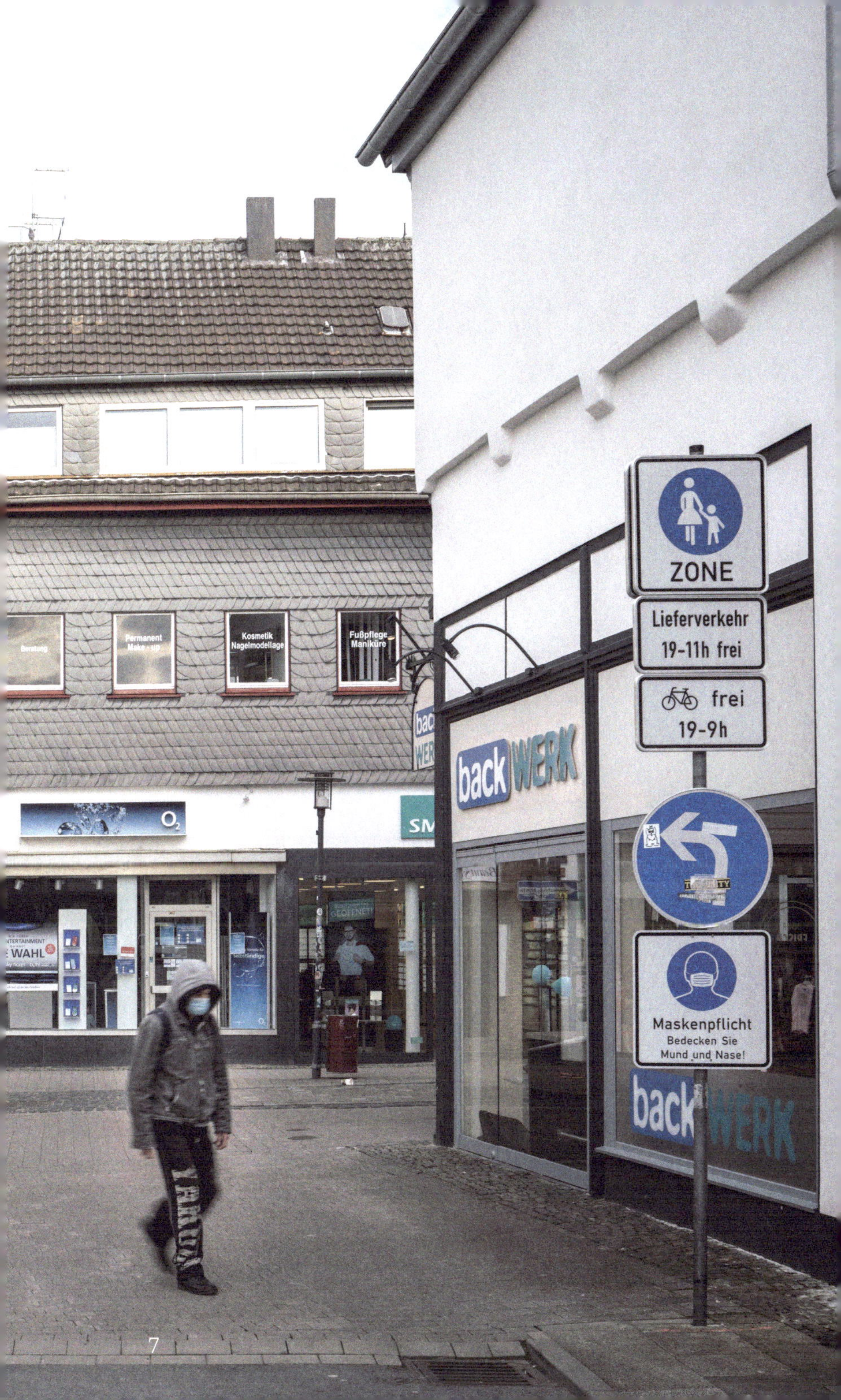
Beratung
Permanent Make - up
Kosmetik Nagelmodellage
Fußpflege Maniküre
O2
ZONE
Lieferverkehr
19-11h frei
frei
19-9h
back WERK
Maskenpflicht
Bedecken Sie
Mund und Nase!
back WERK

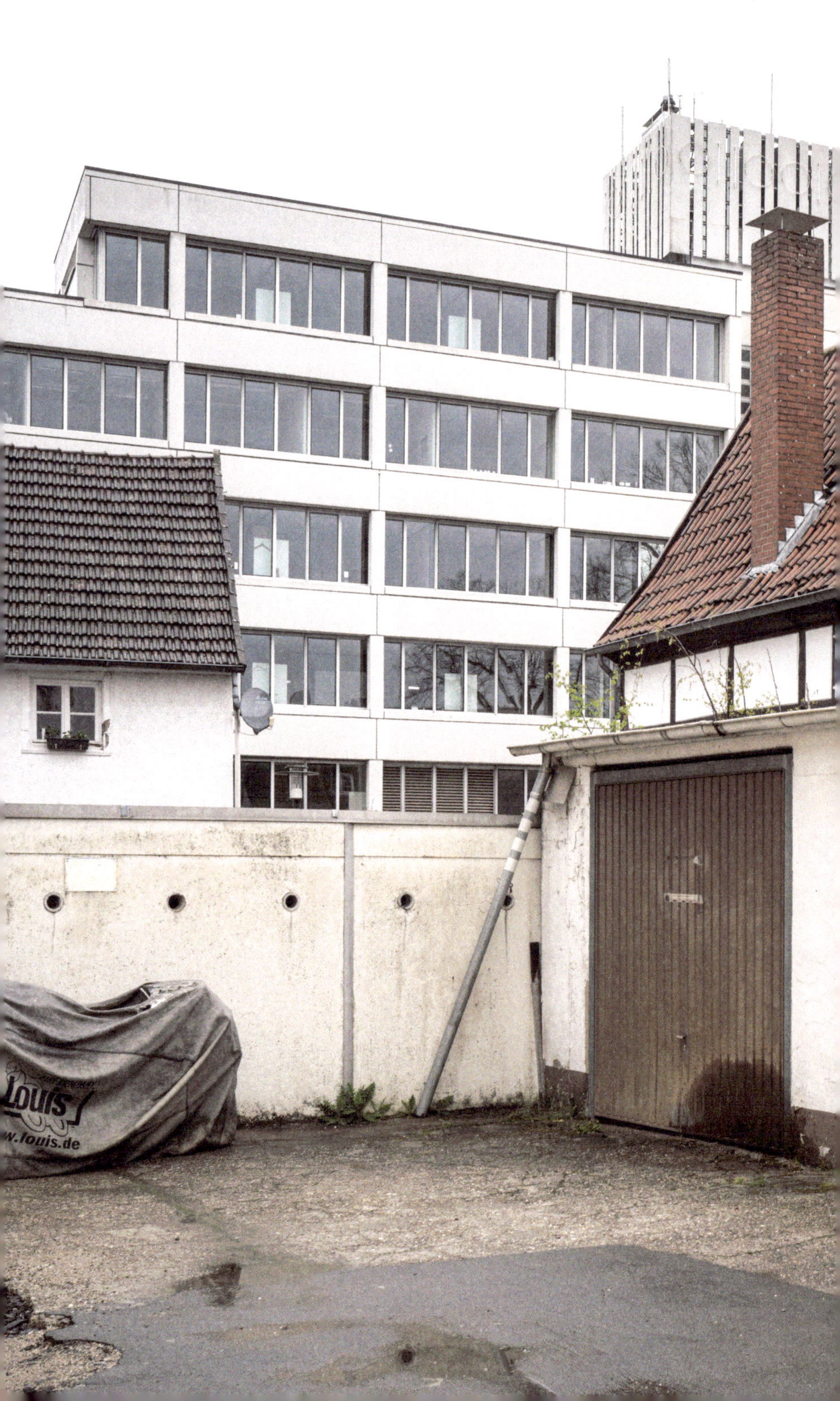
Louis
w.louis.de

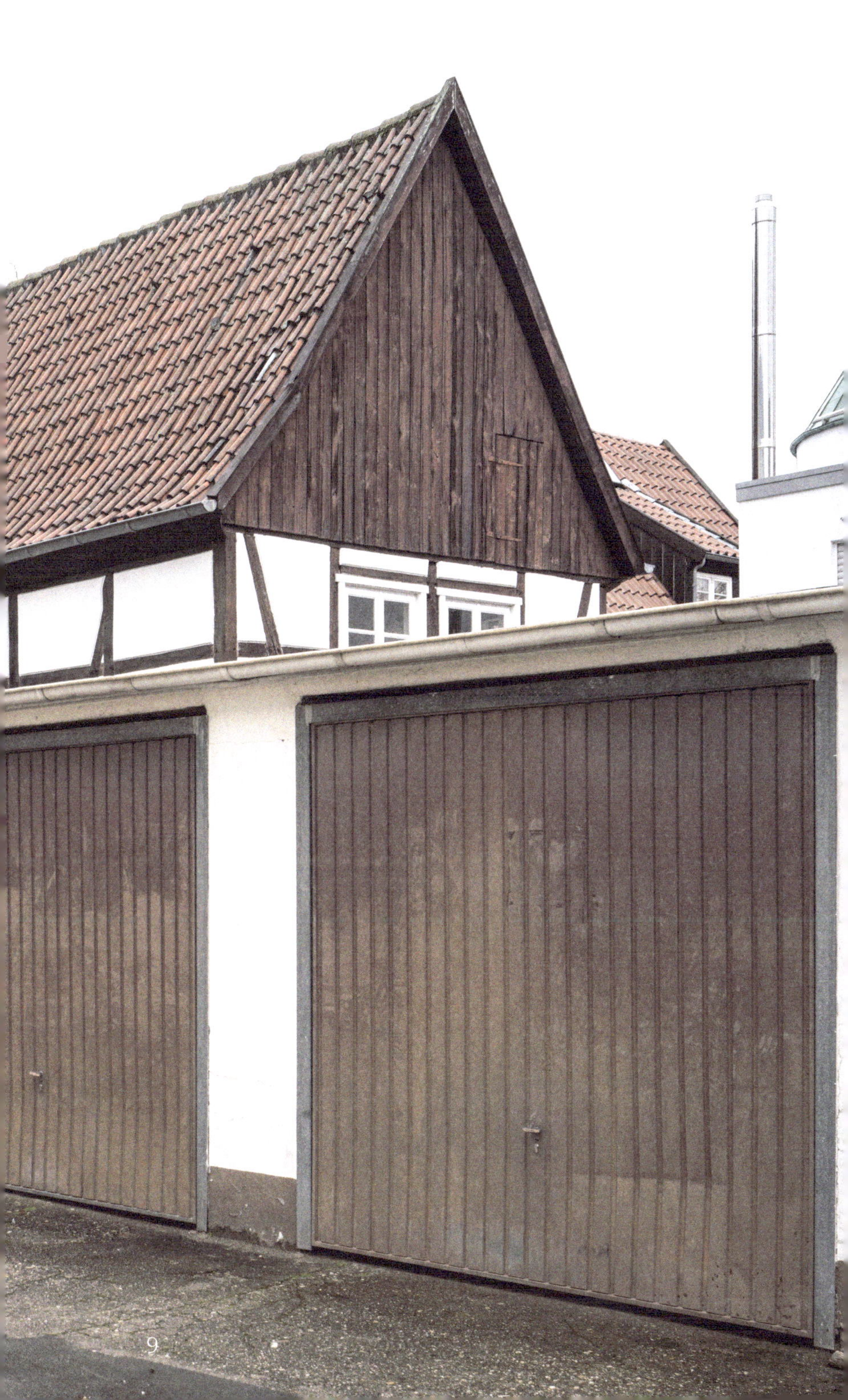

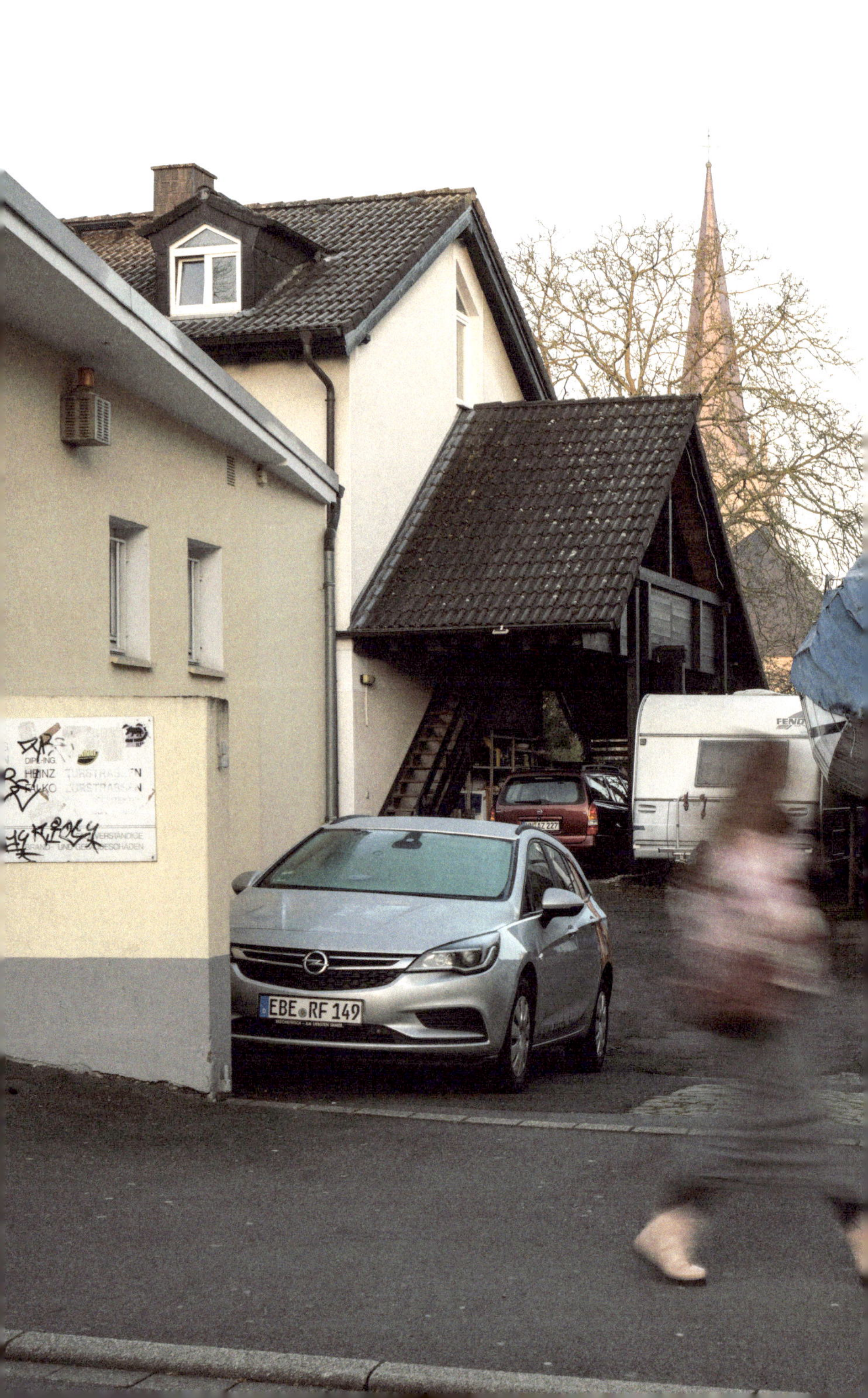
EBE RF 149

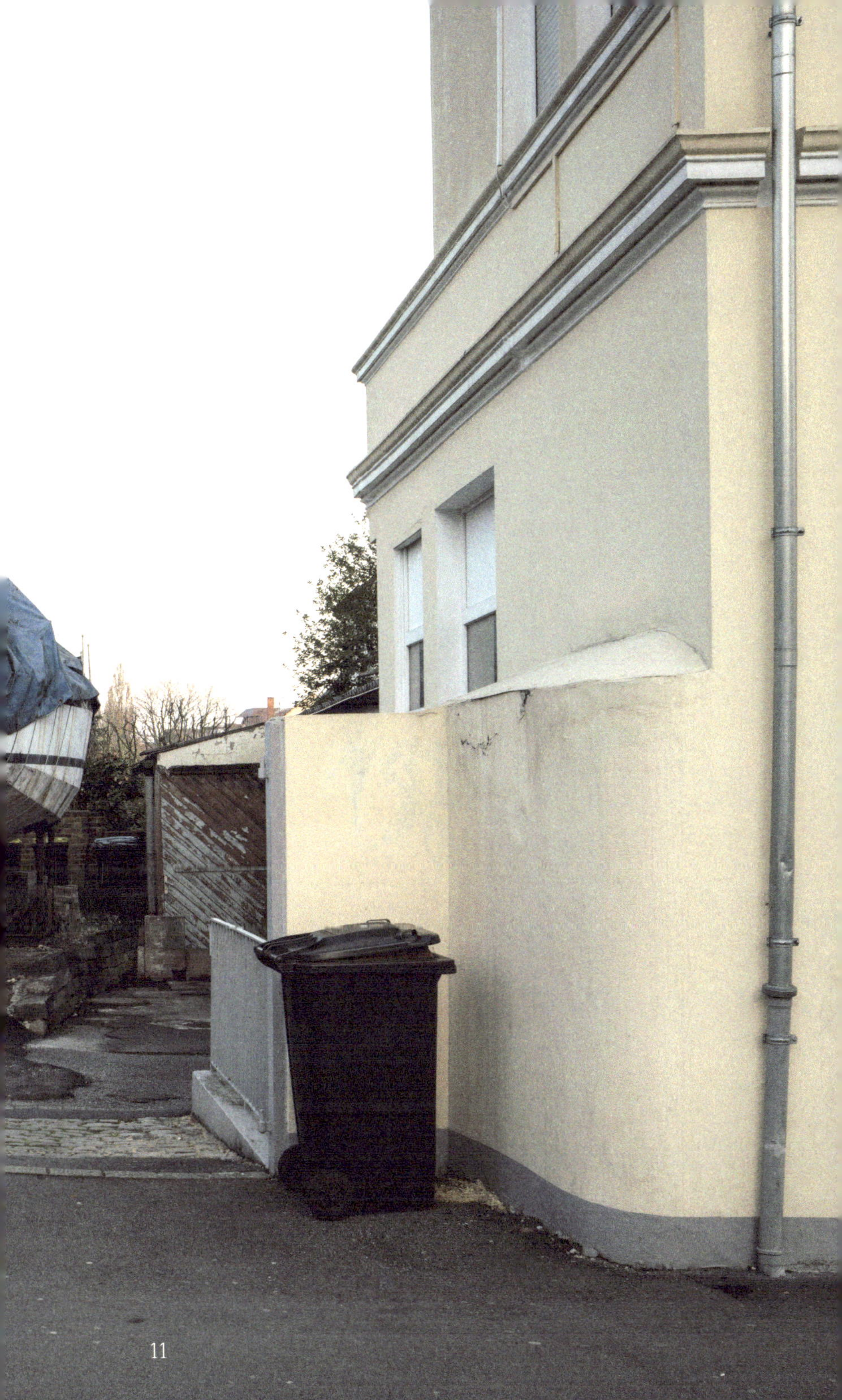

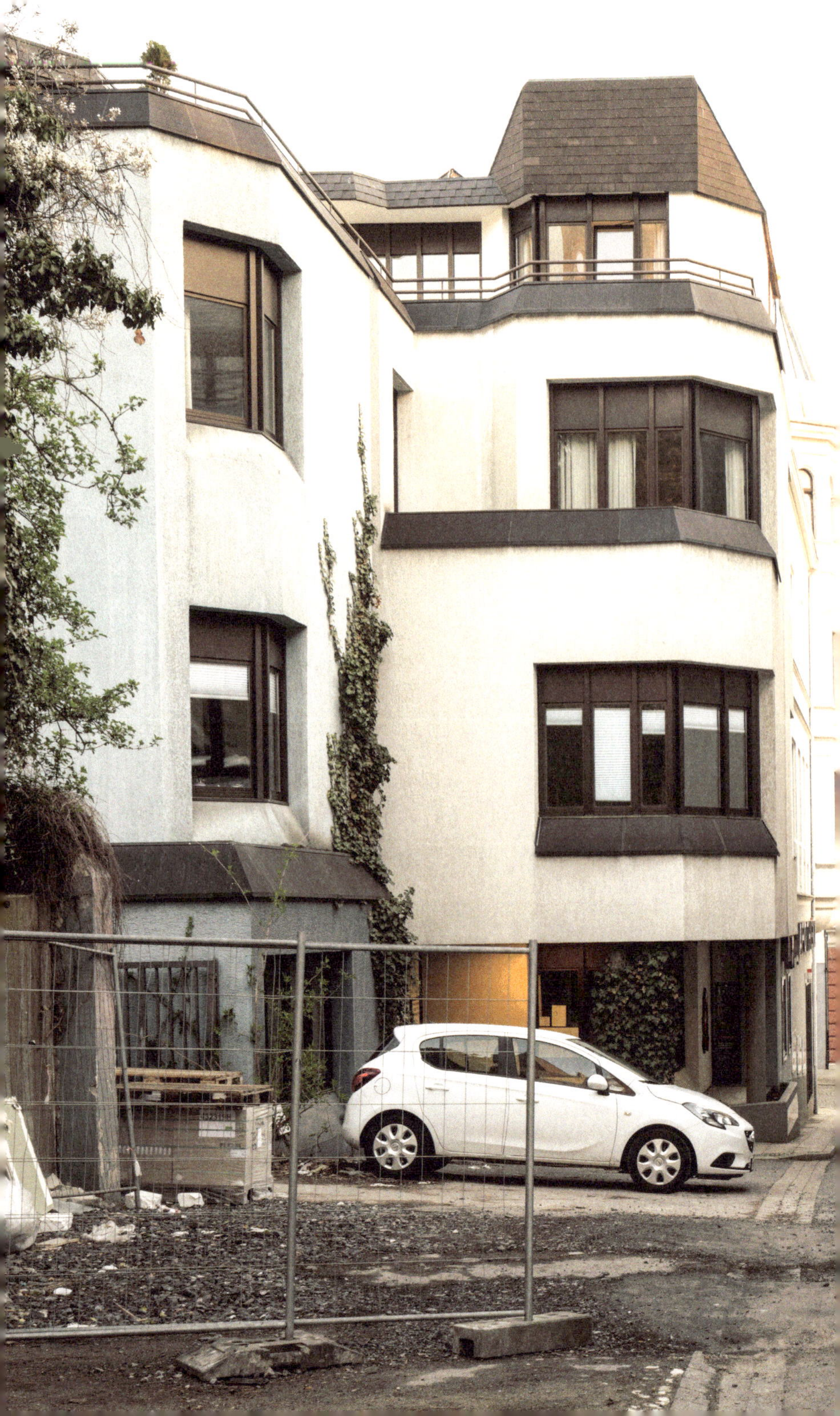

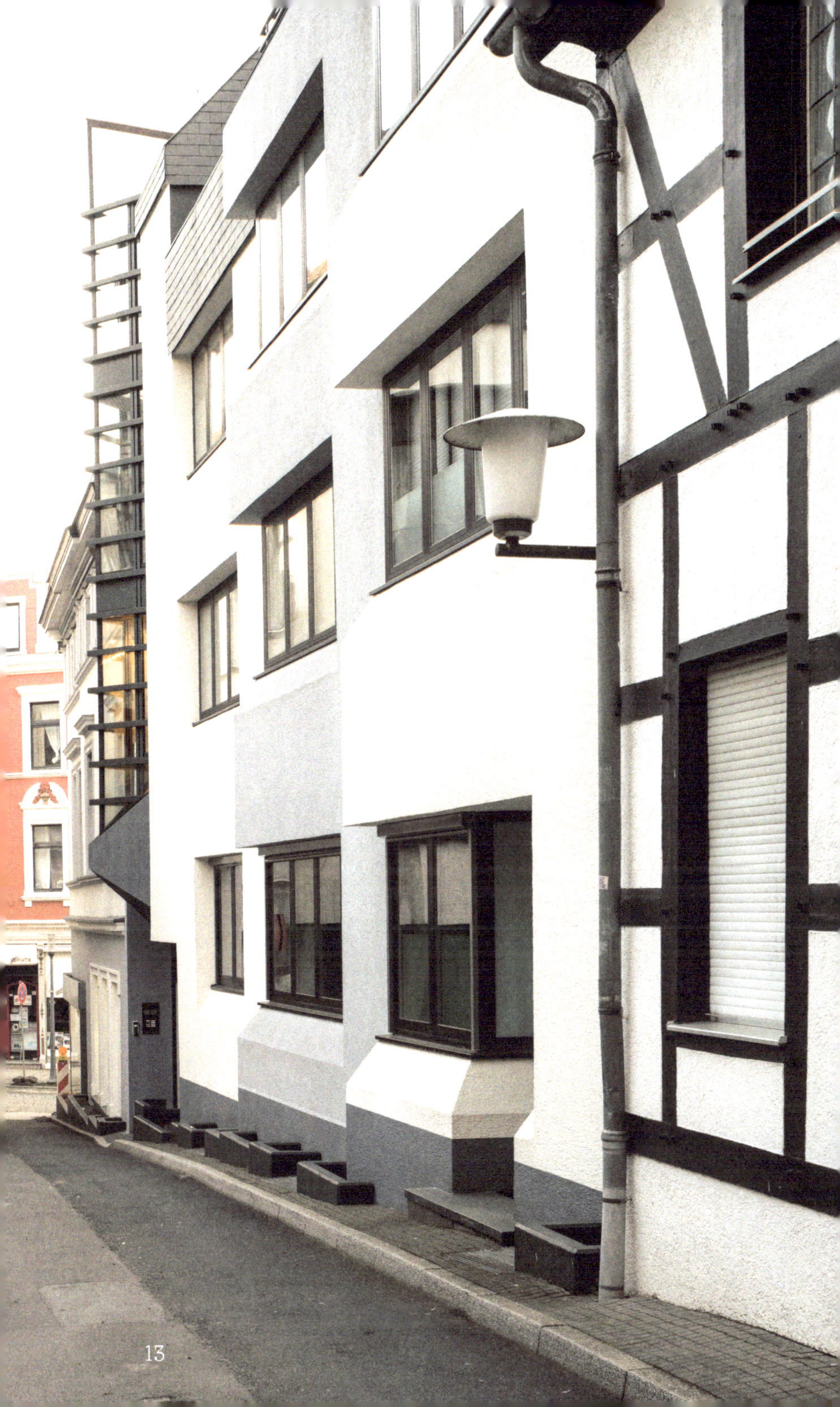

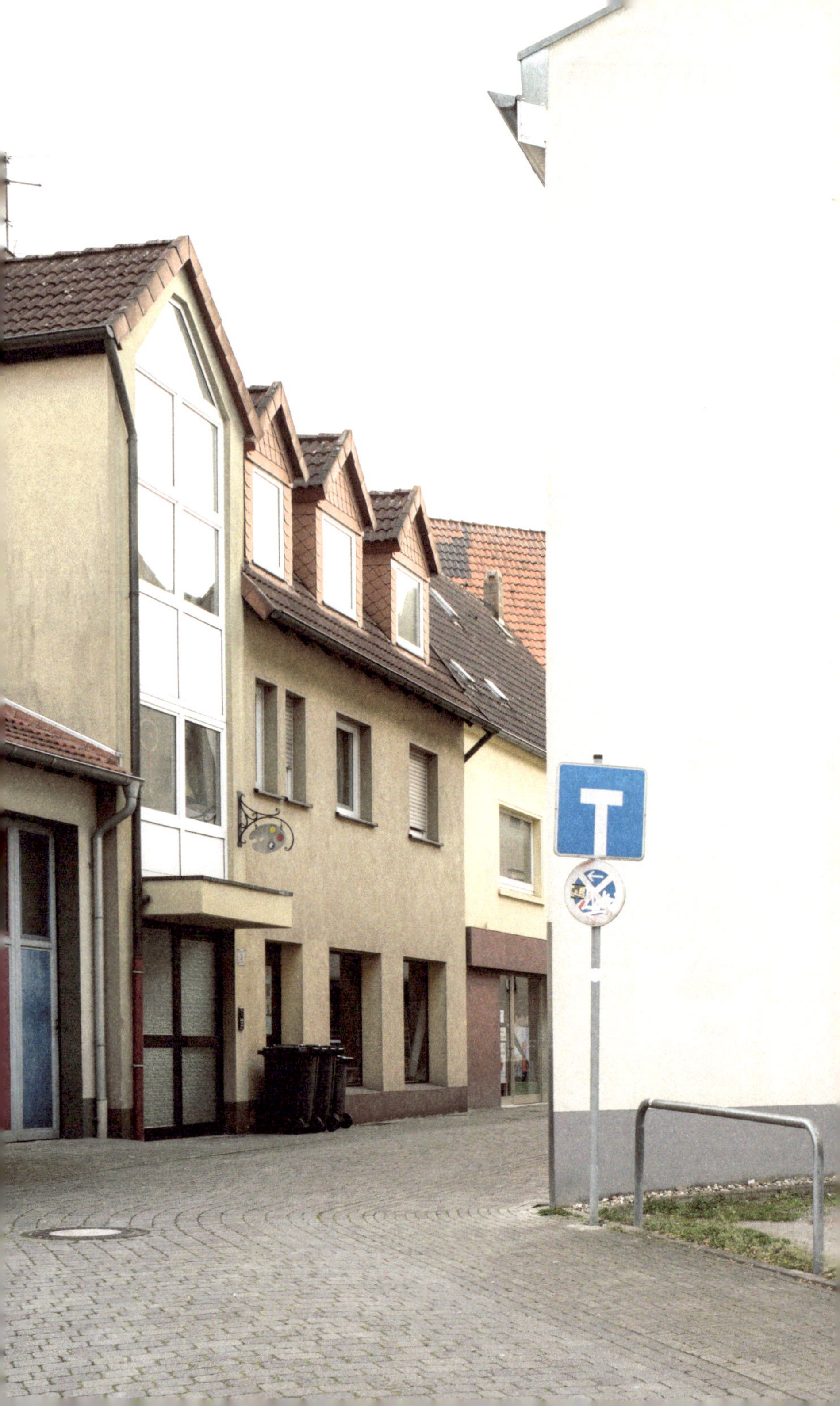

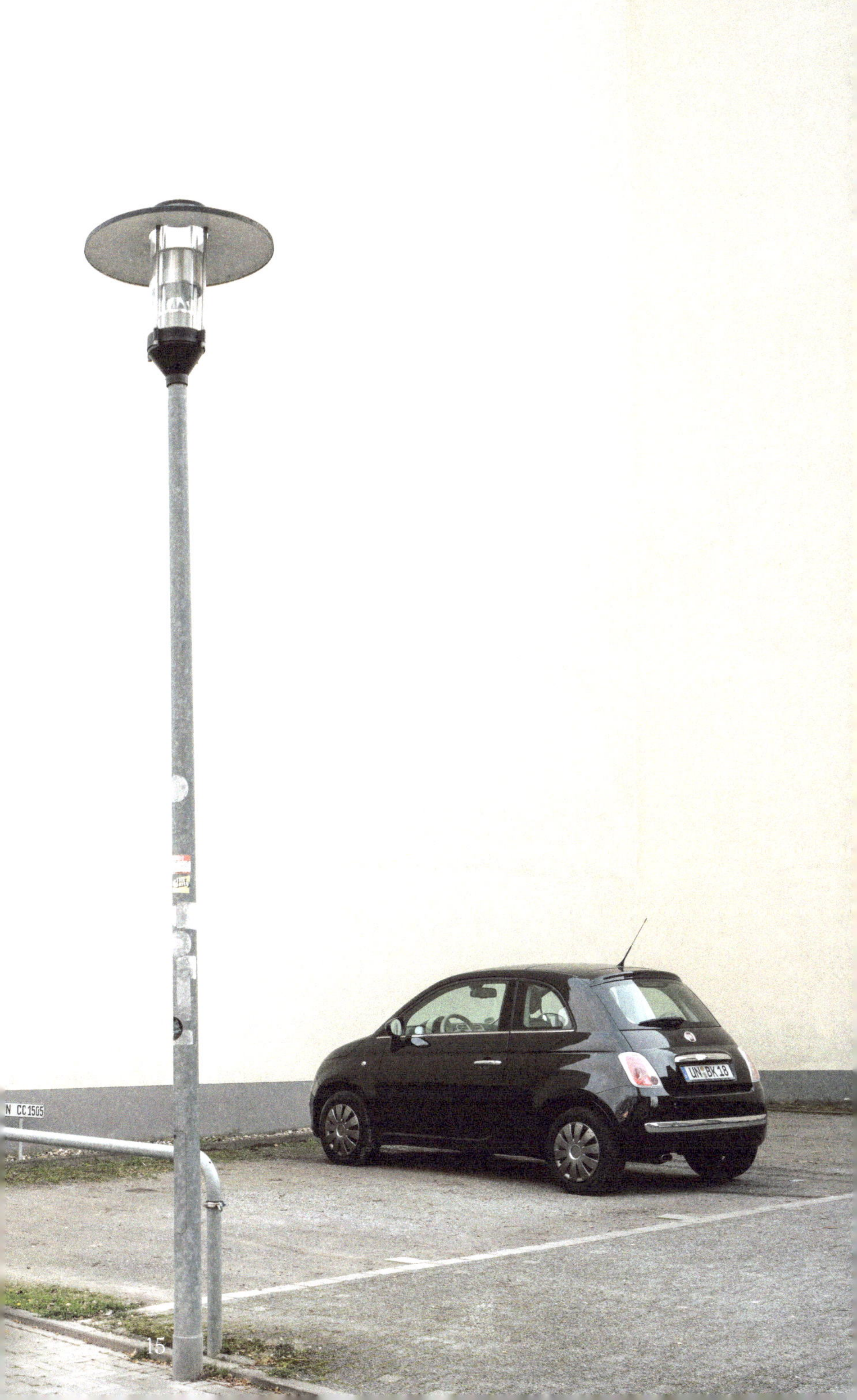
N CC 1505
UN BK 18

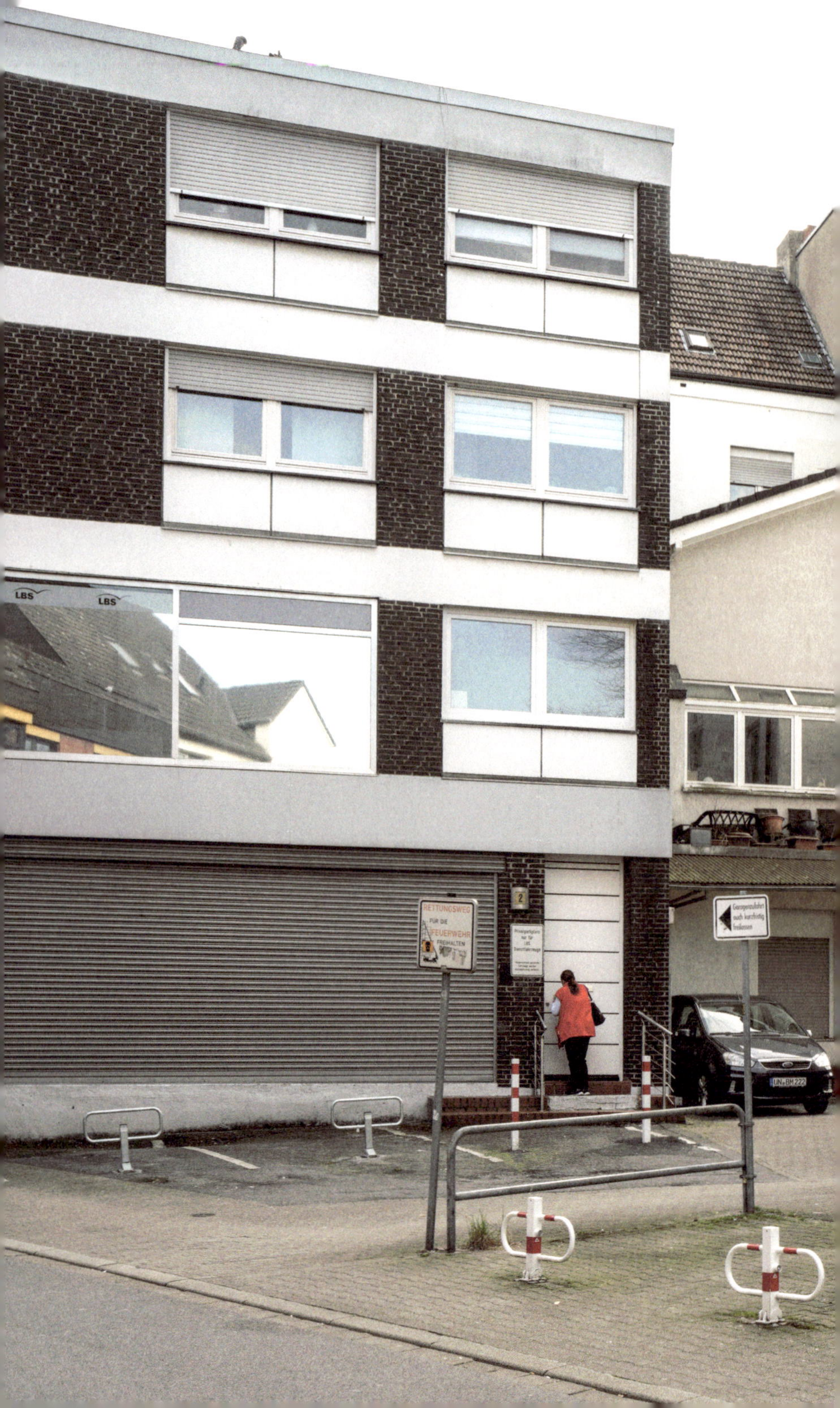
LBS
LBS
RETTUNGSWEG
FÜR DIE
FEUERWEHR
FREIHALTEN
2
Garagenzufahrt
auch kurzfristig
freilassen
UN BM 222

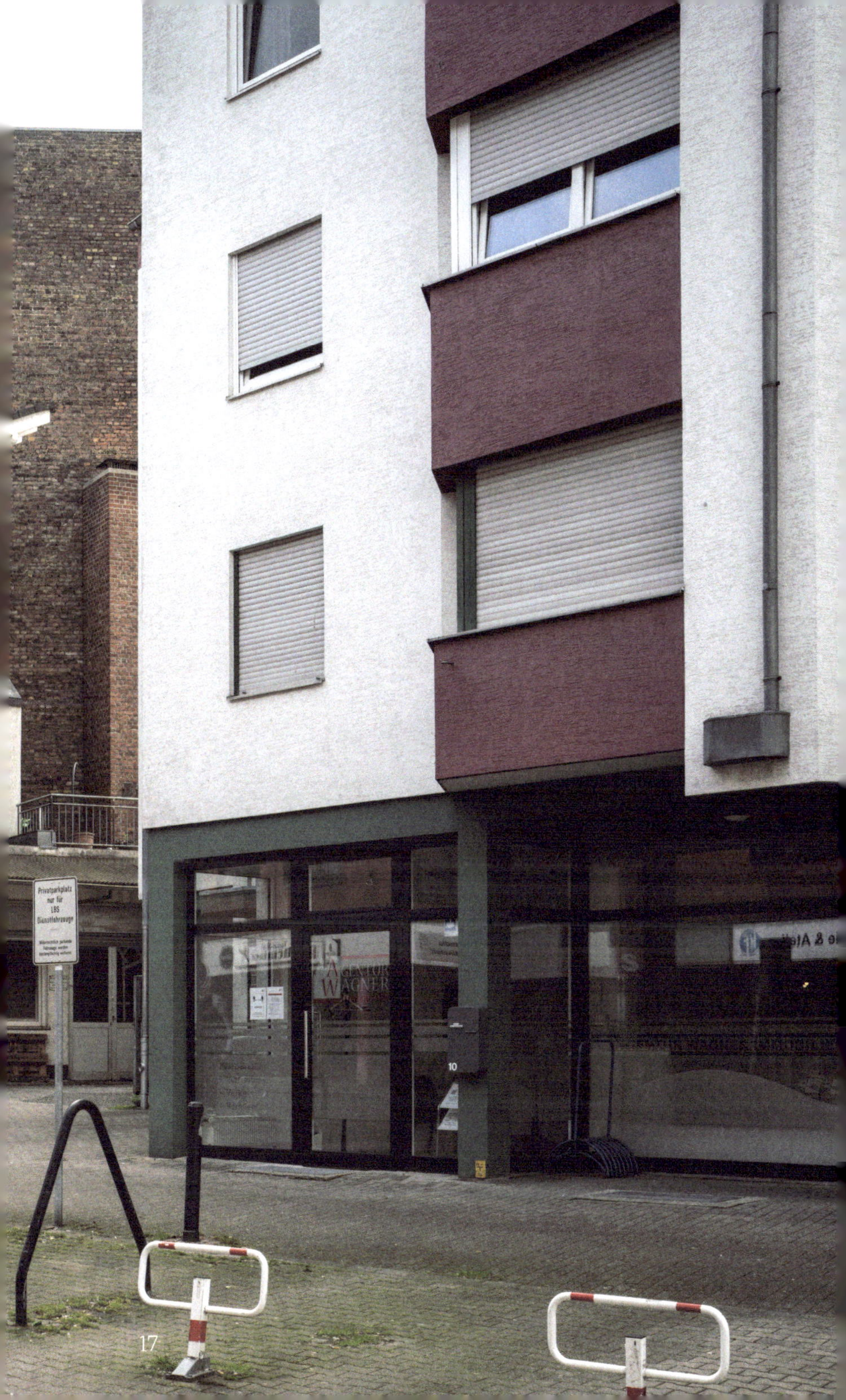
Privatparkplatz
nur für
LBS
Dienstfahrzeuge
10

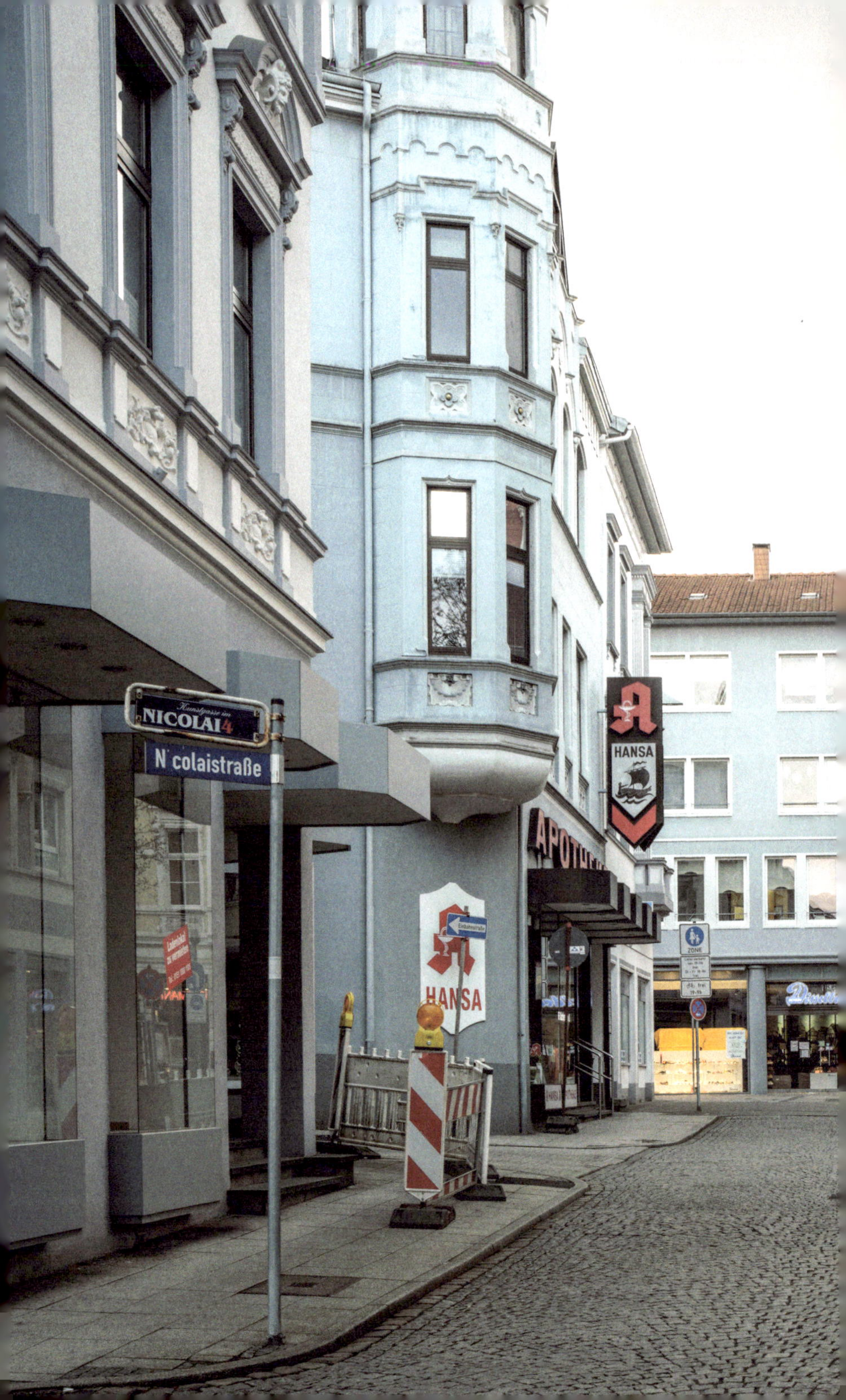
Kunstgasse im
NICOLAI 4
N colaistraße
HANSA
HANSA

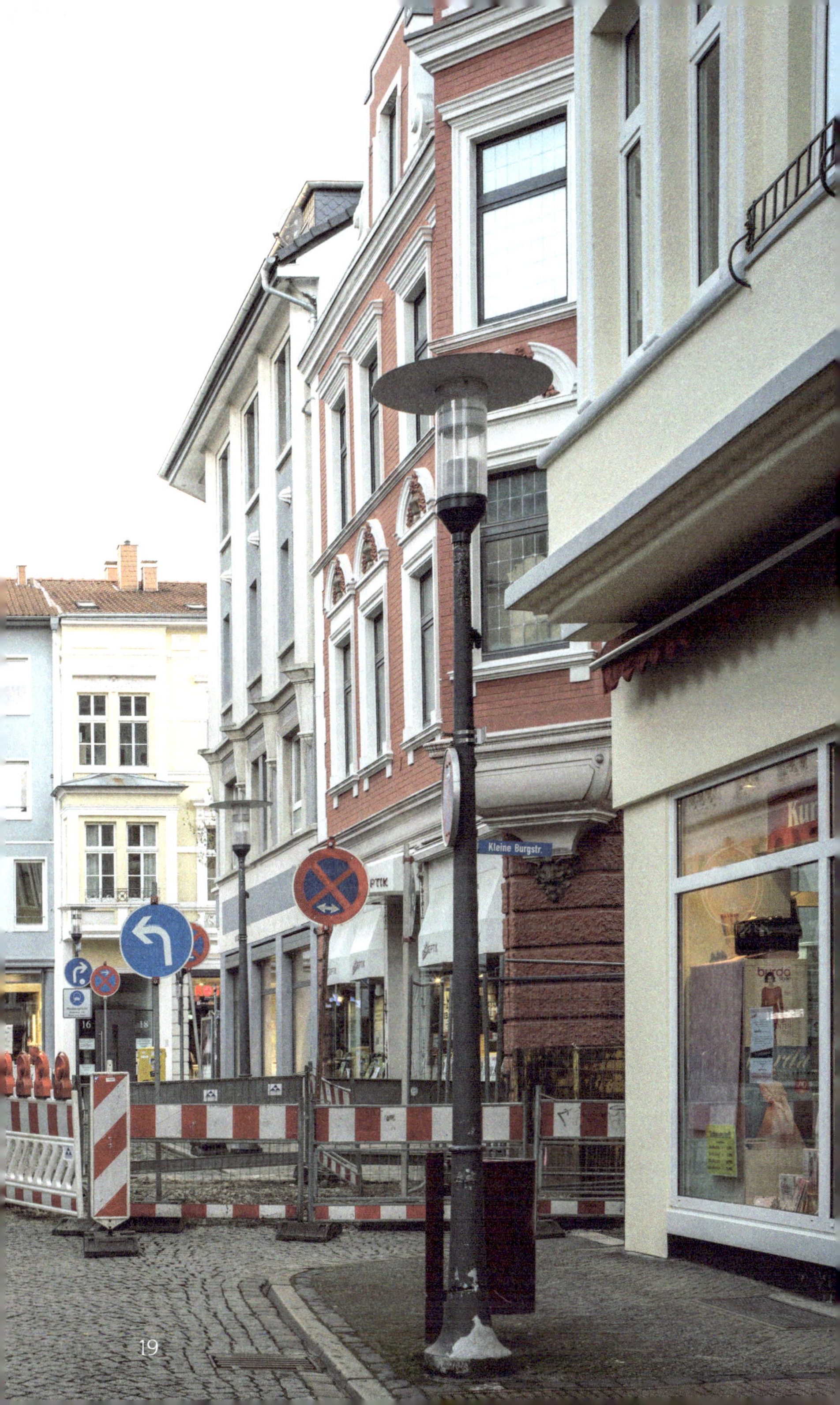
Kleine Burgstr.

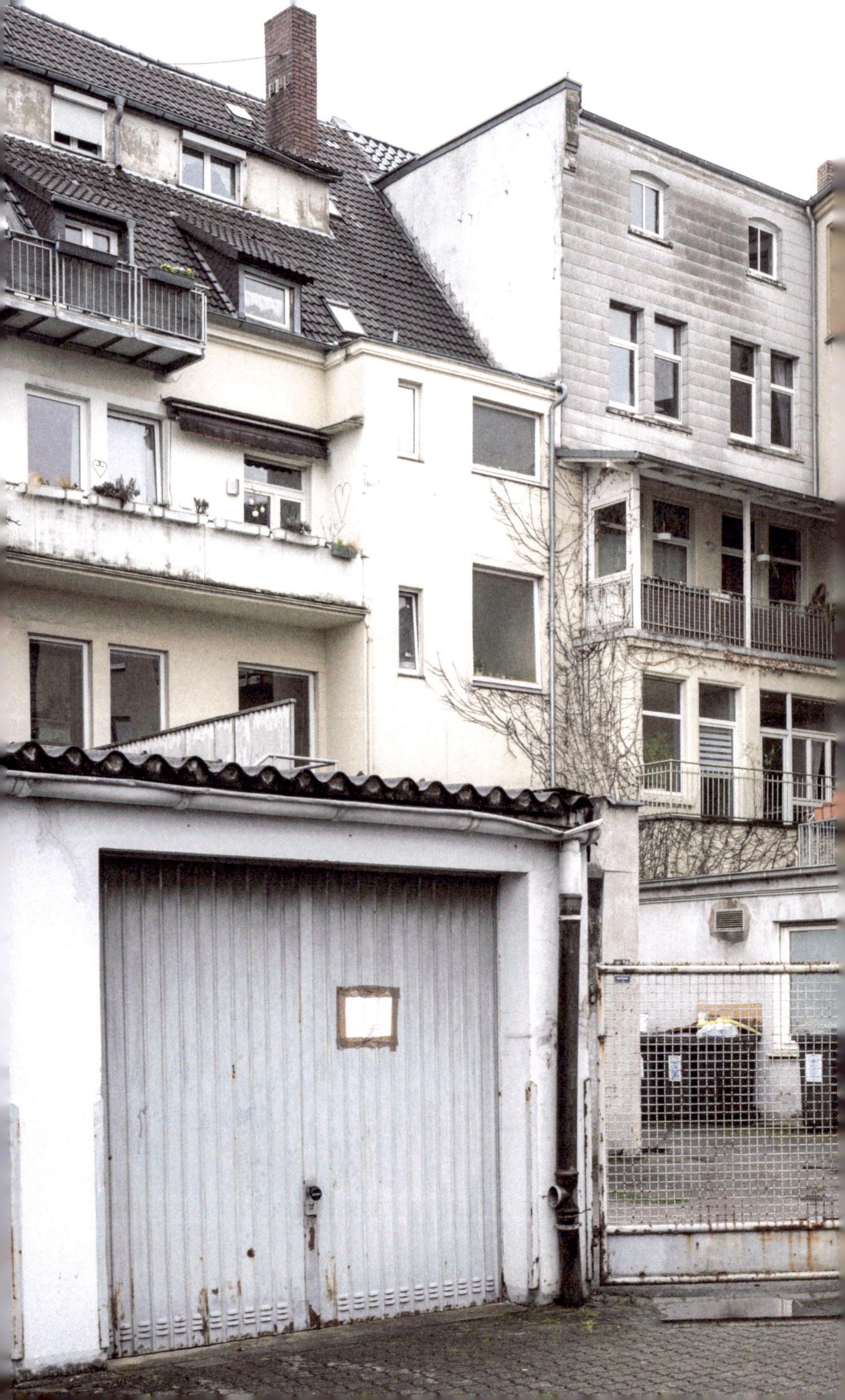

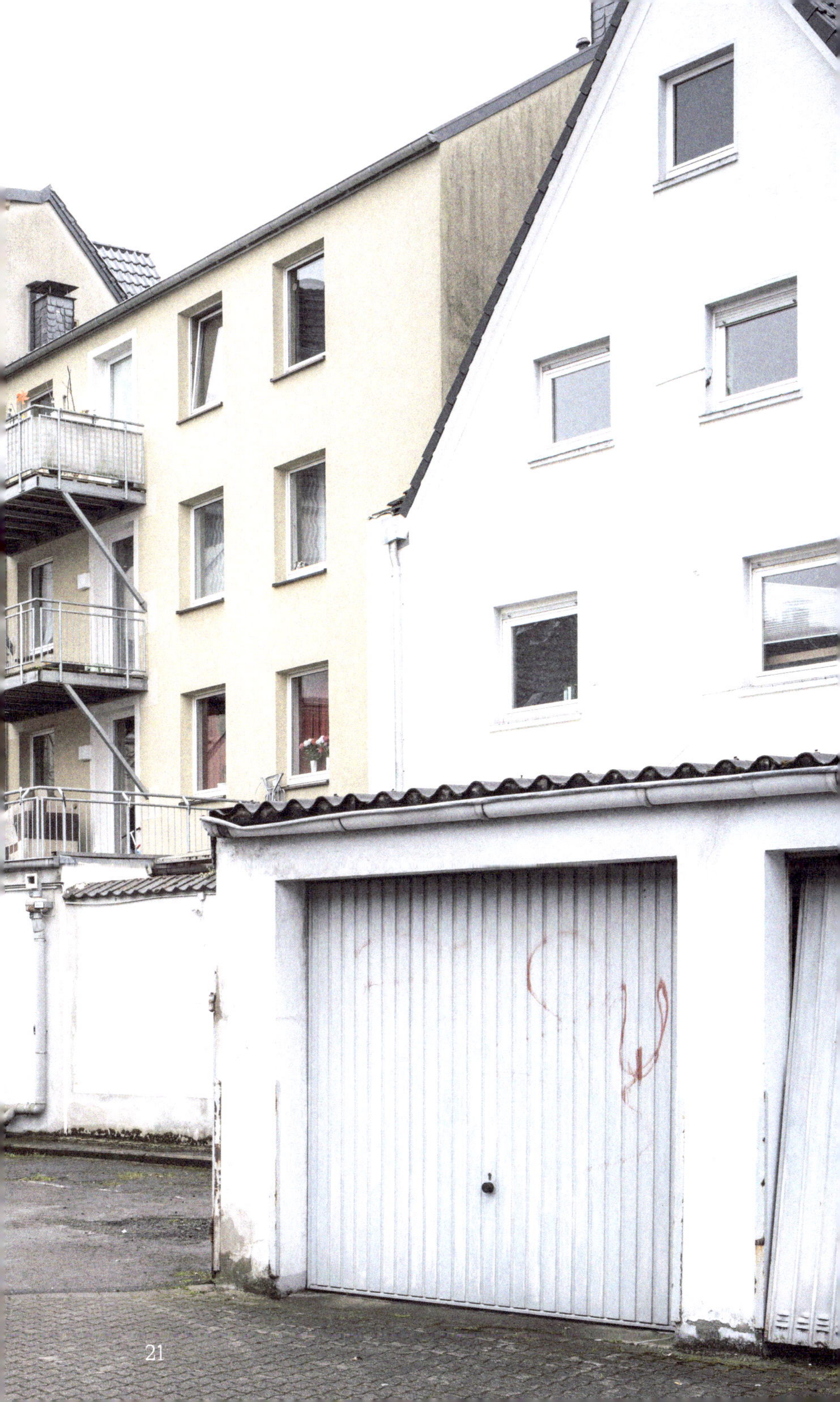

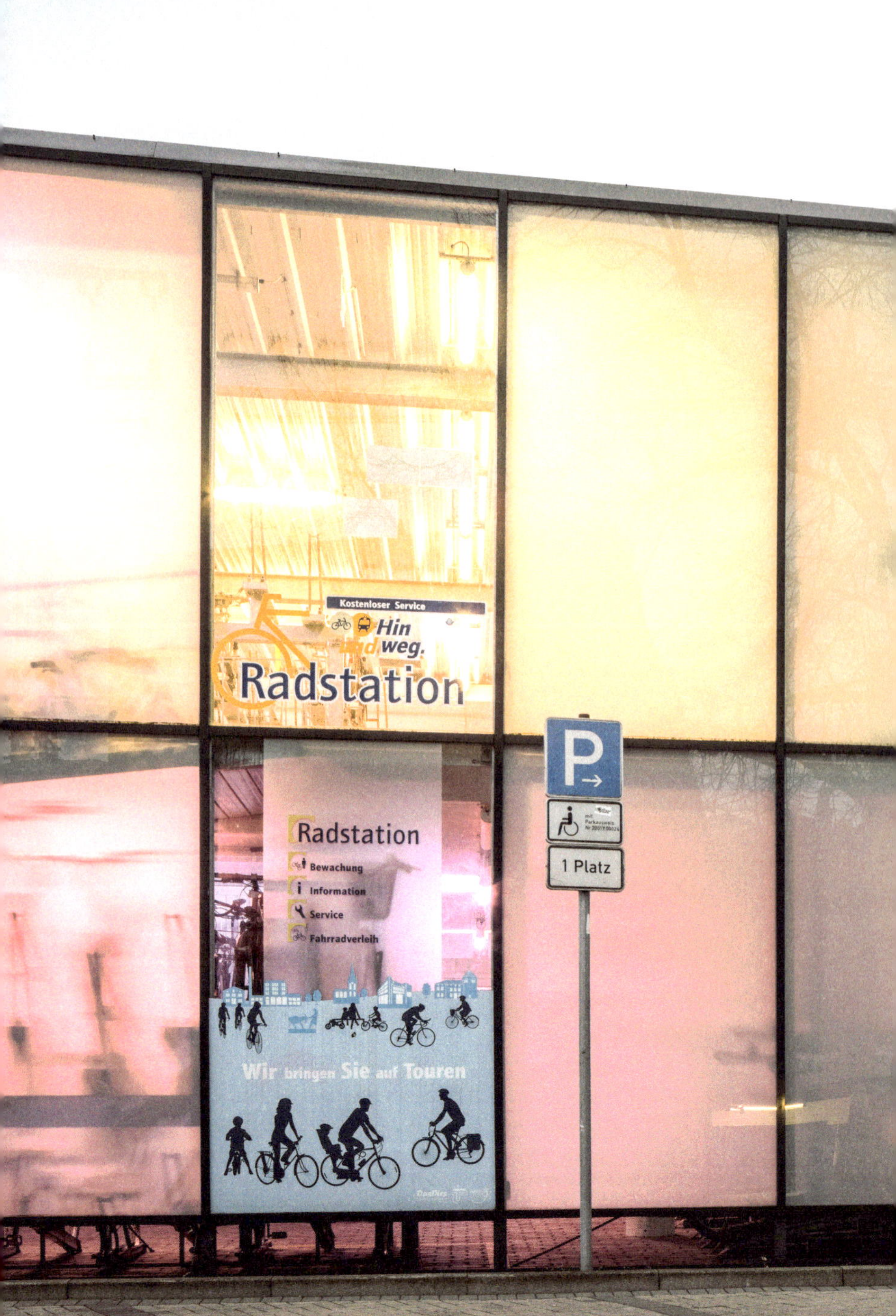
Kostenloser Service
Hin
weg.
Radstation
P
1 Platz
Radstation
Bewachung
Information
Service
Fahrradverleih
Wir bringen Sie auf Touren

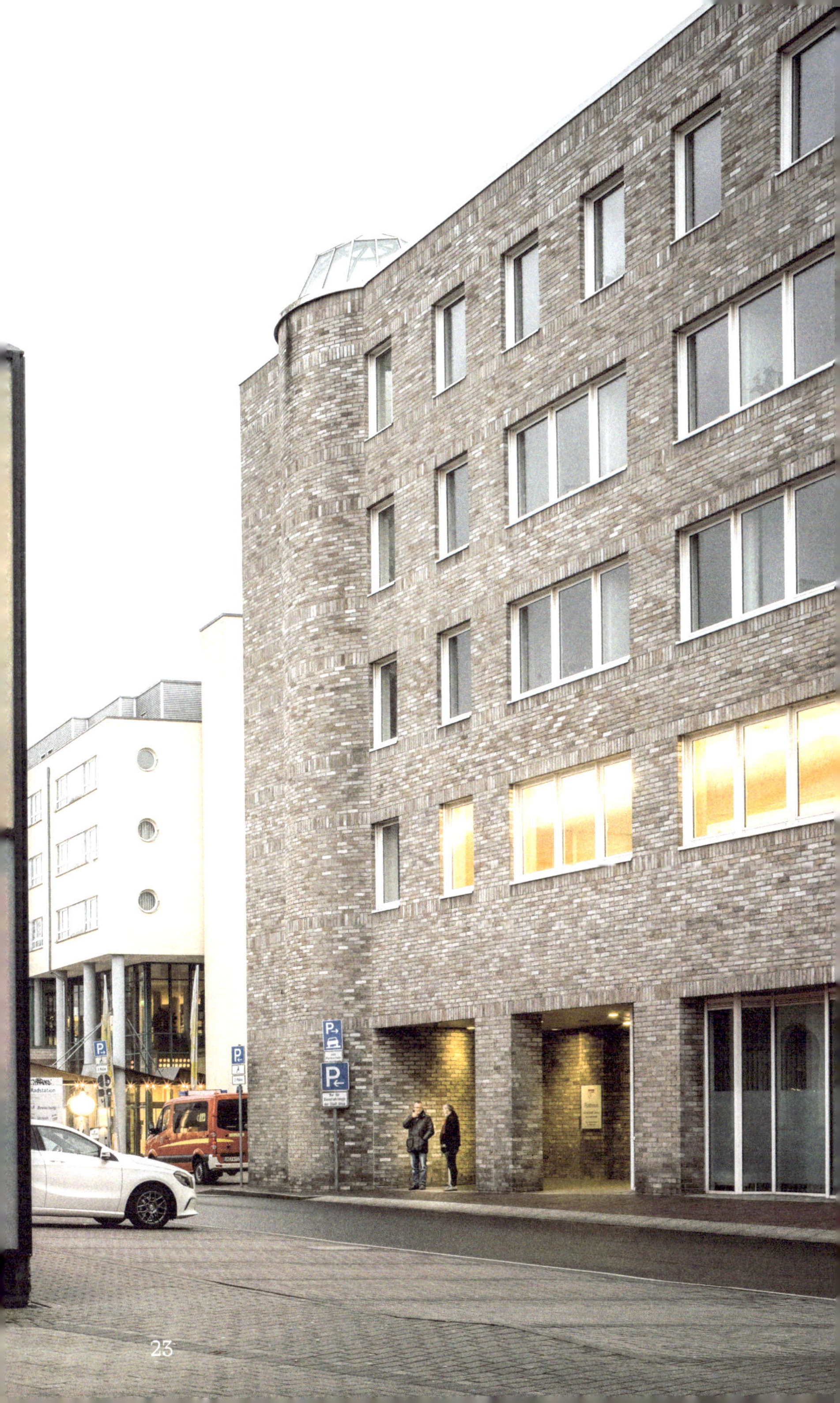
Radstation

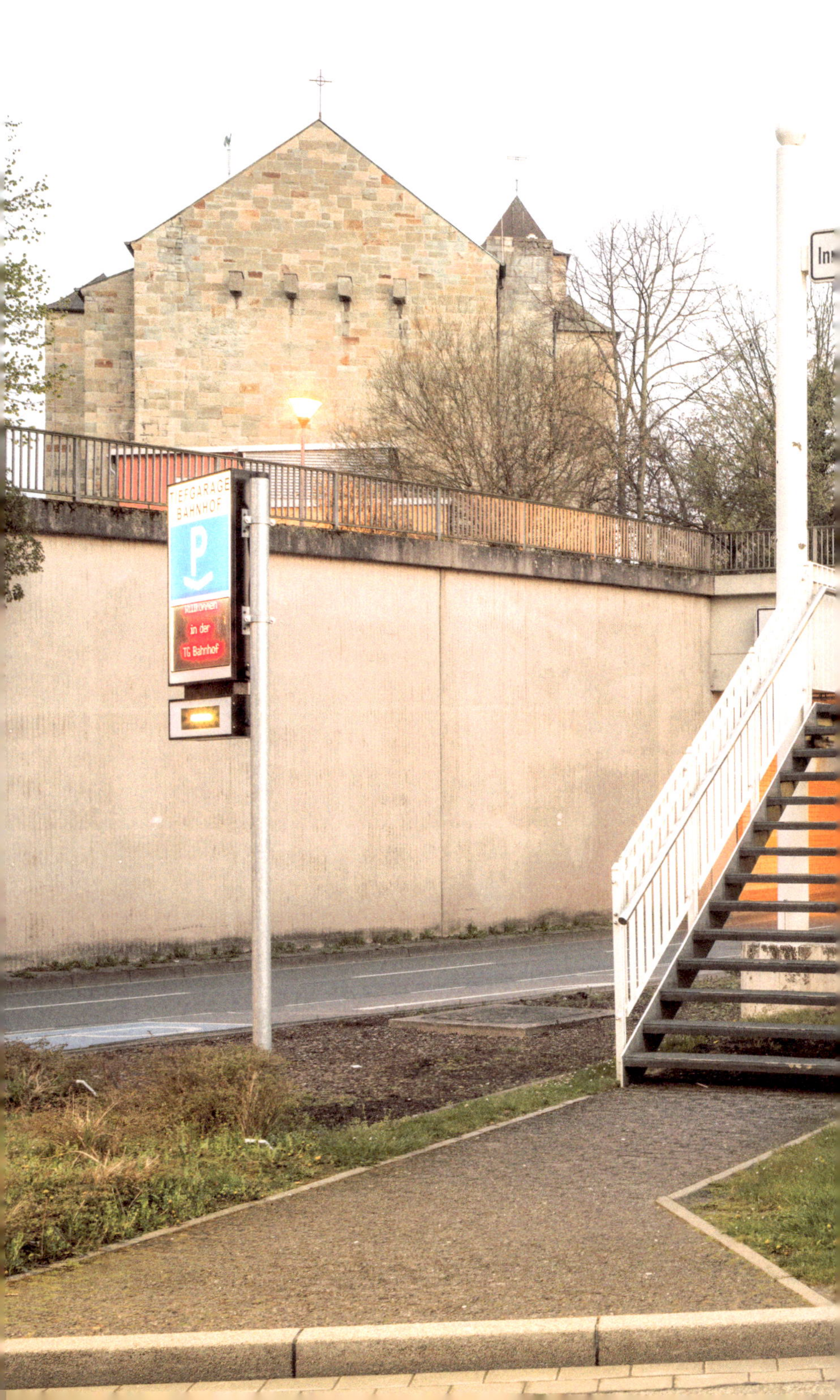
TIEFGARAGE
BAHNHOF
P
in der
TG Bahnhof

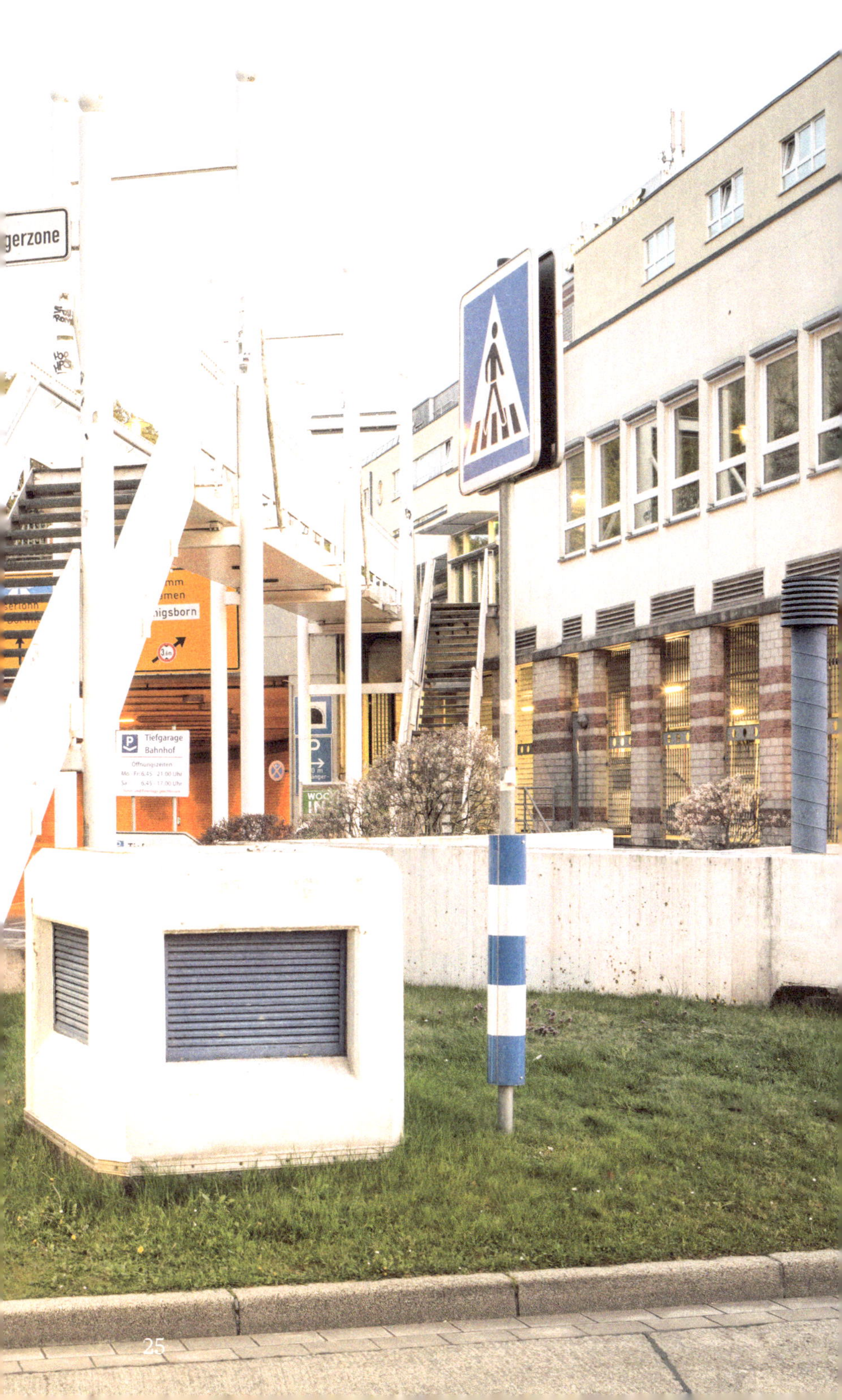
gerzone
nigsborn
Tiefgarage
Bahnhof
Öffnungszeiten

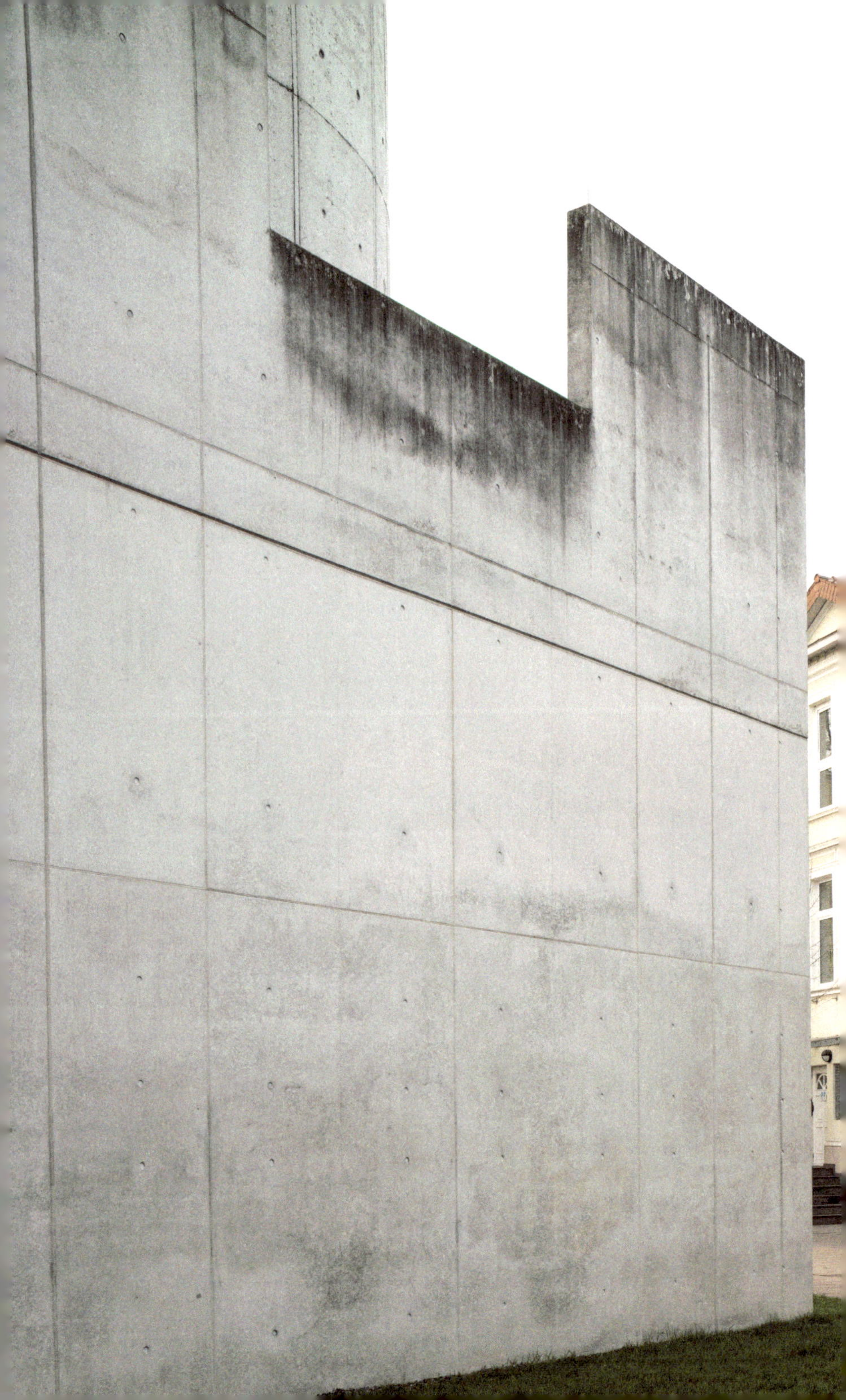

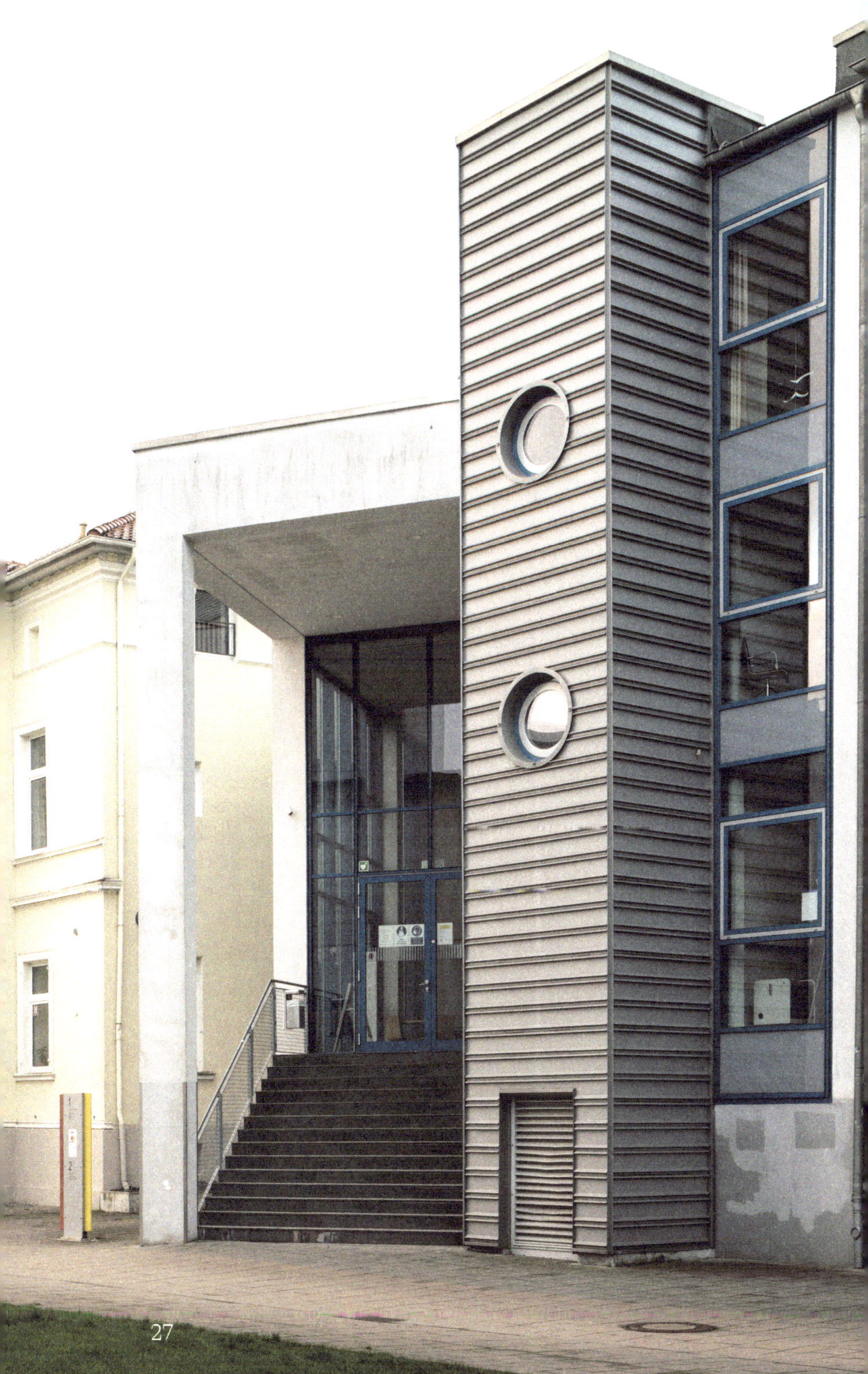

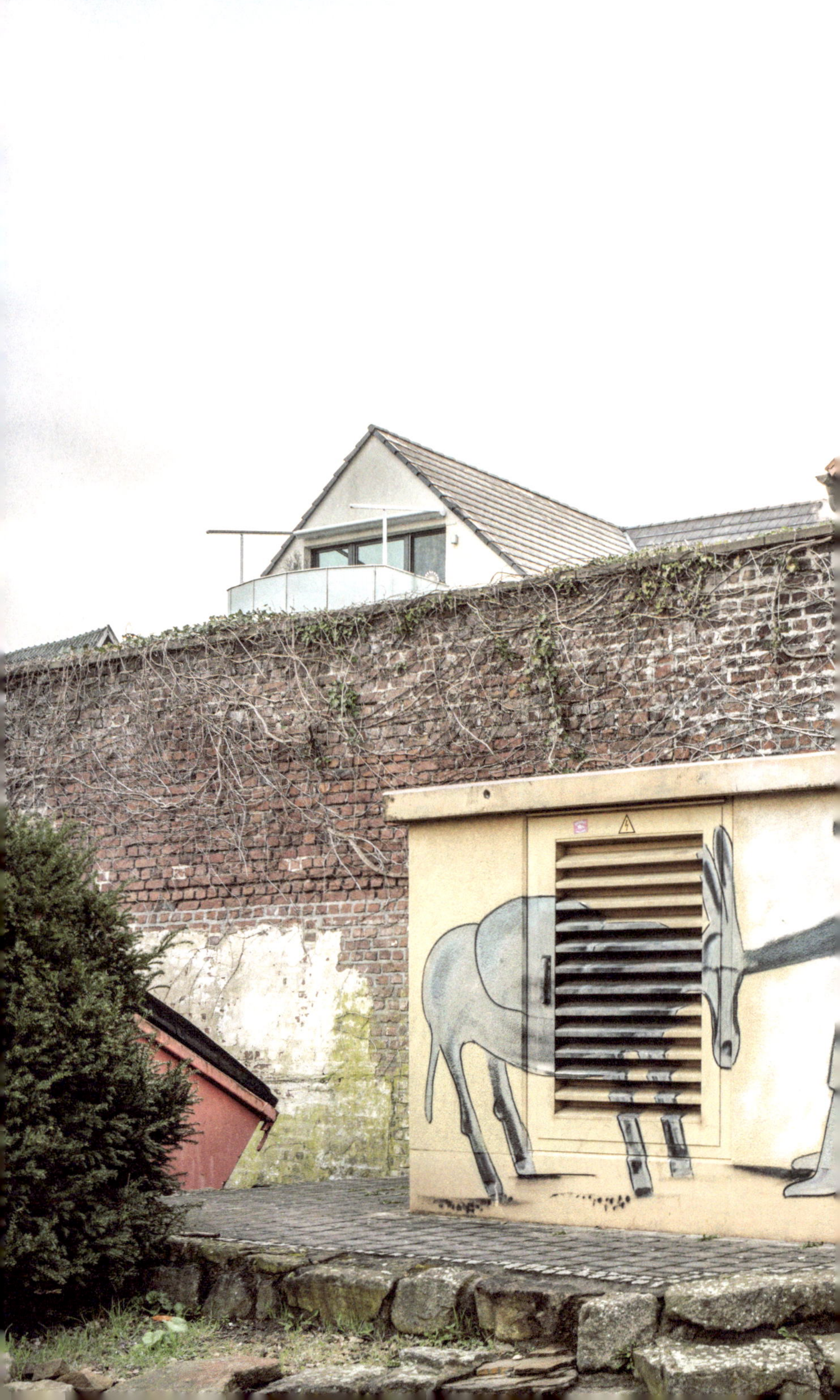

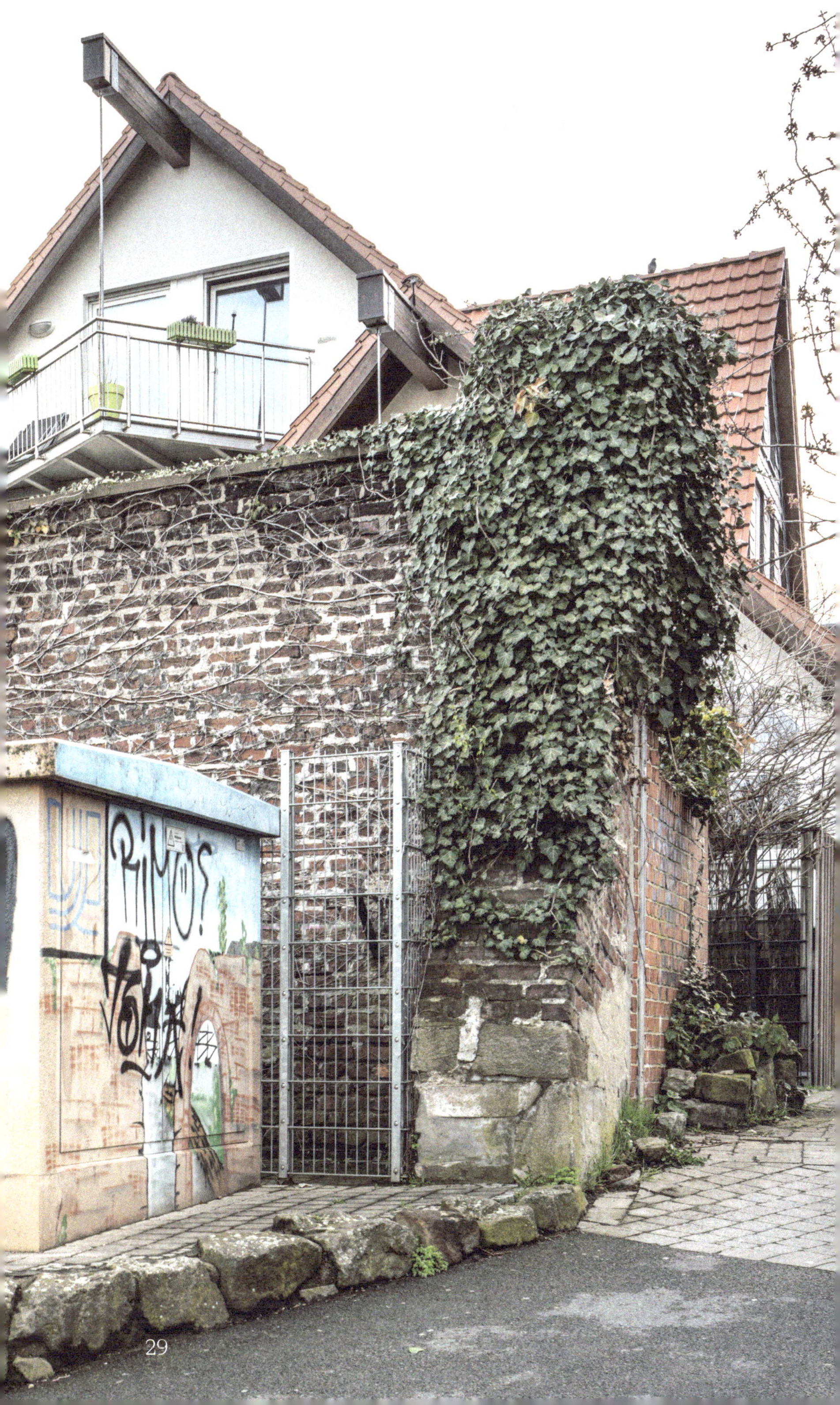

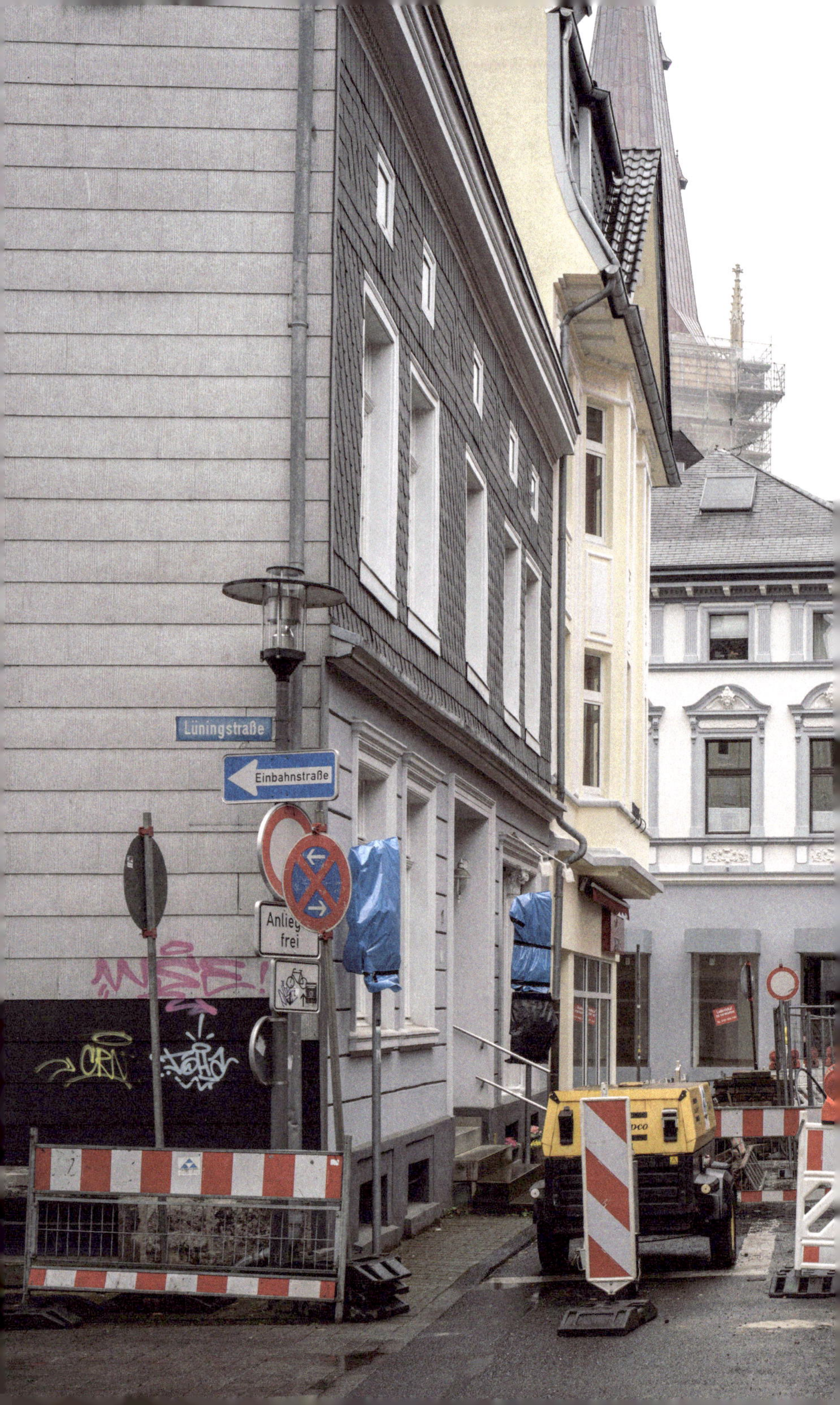
Lüningstraße
Einbahnstraße
Anlieg
frei

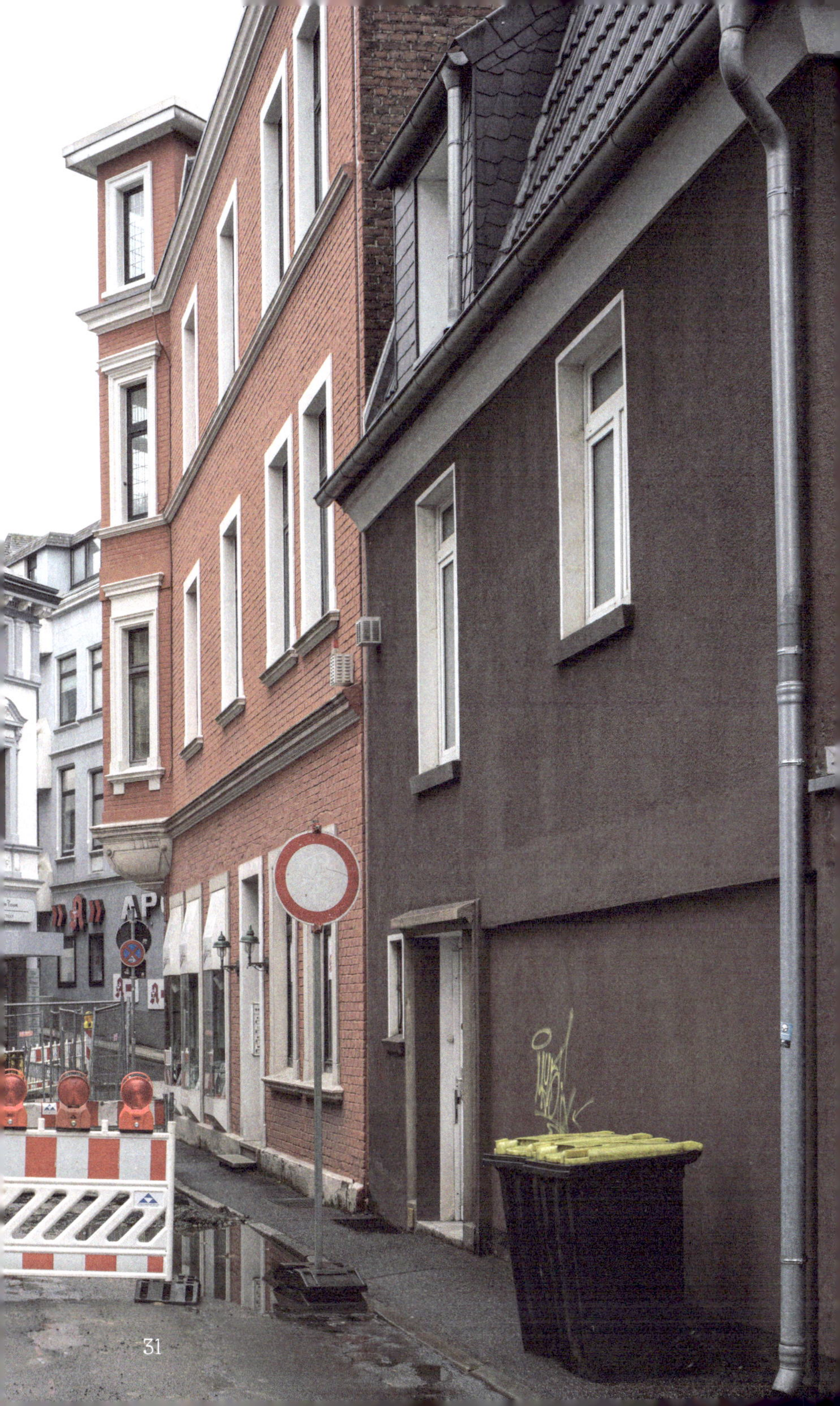

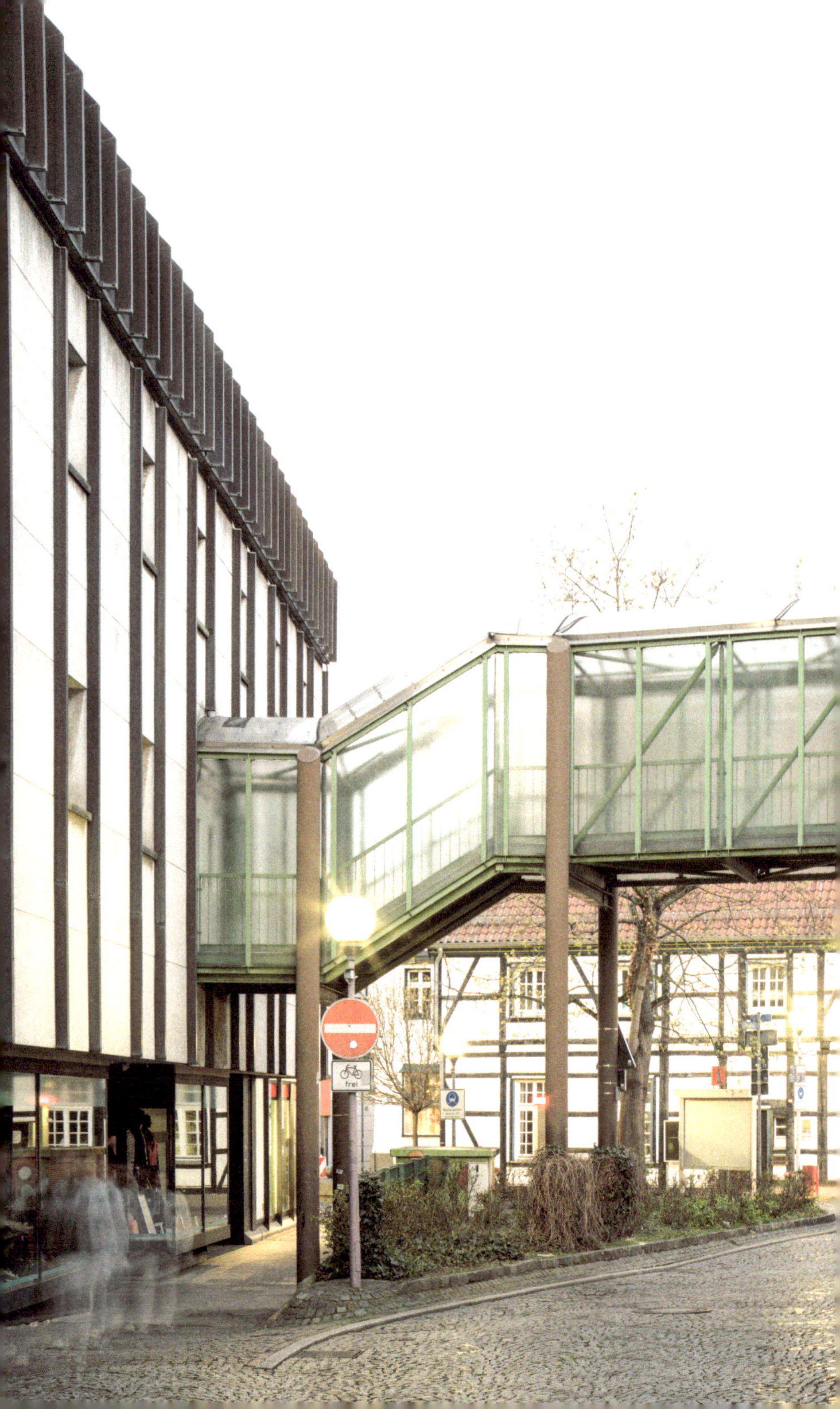
frei

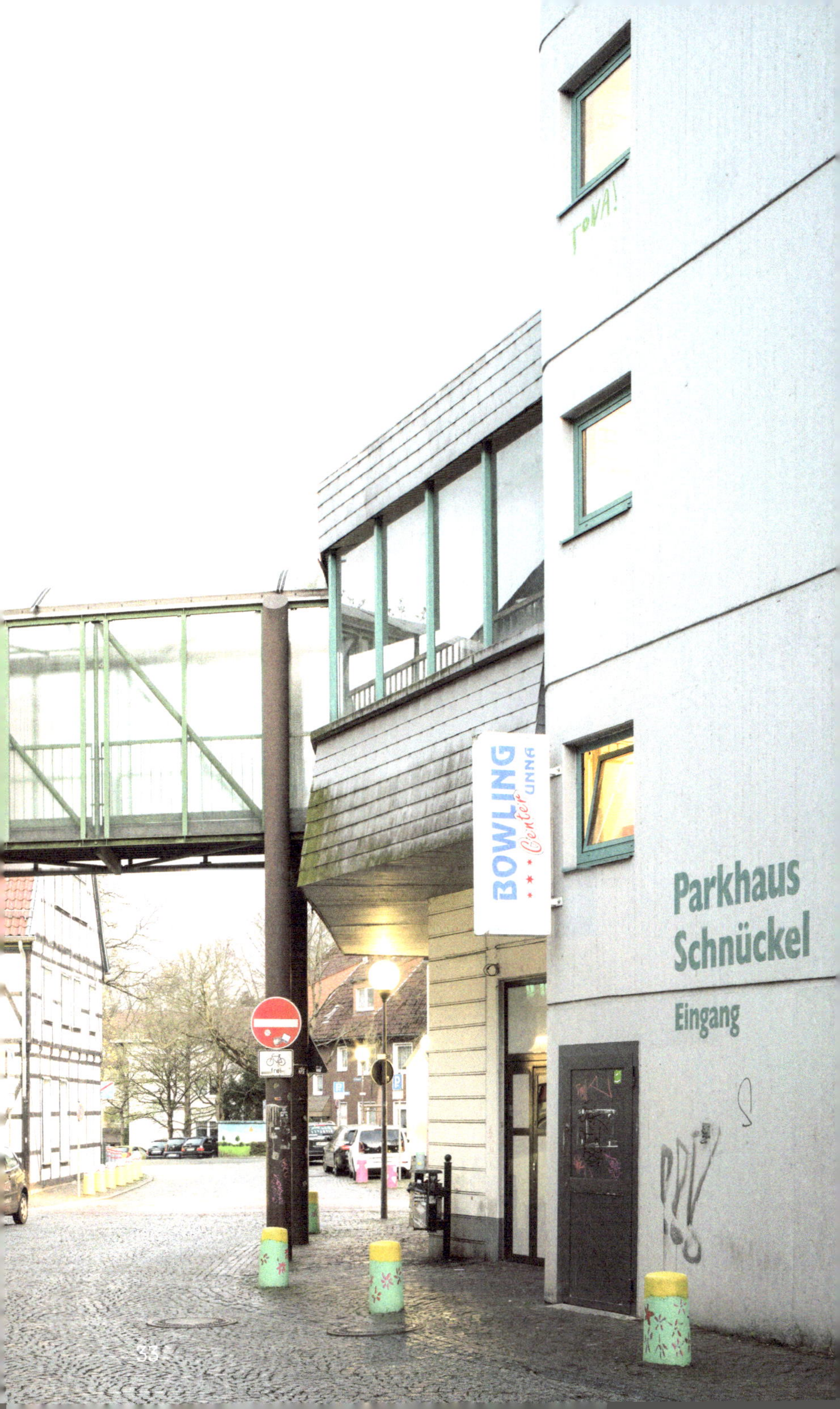
BOWLING
Center
UNNA
Parkhaus
Schnückel
Eingang

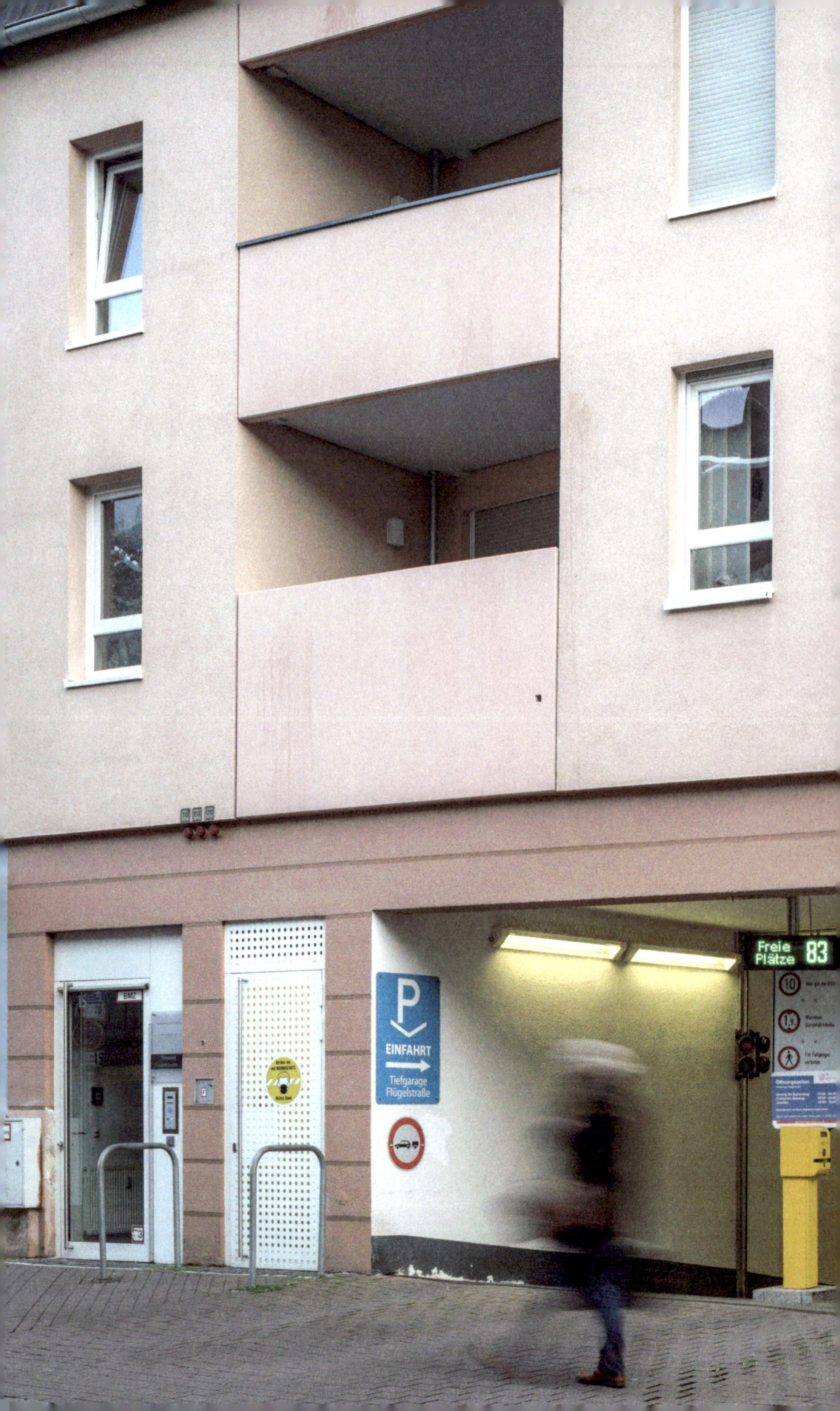
Freie
Plätze
83
P
EINFAHRT
Tiefgarage
Flügelstraße
BMZ
10

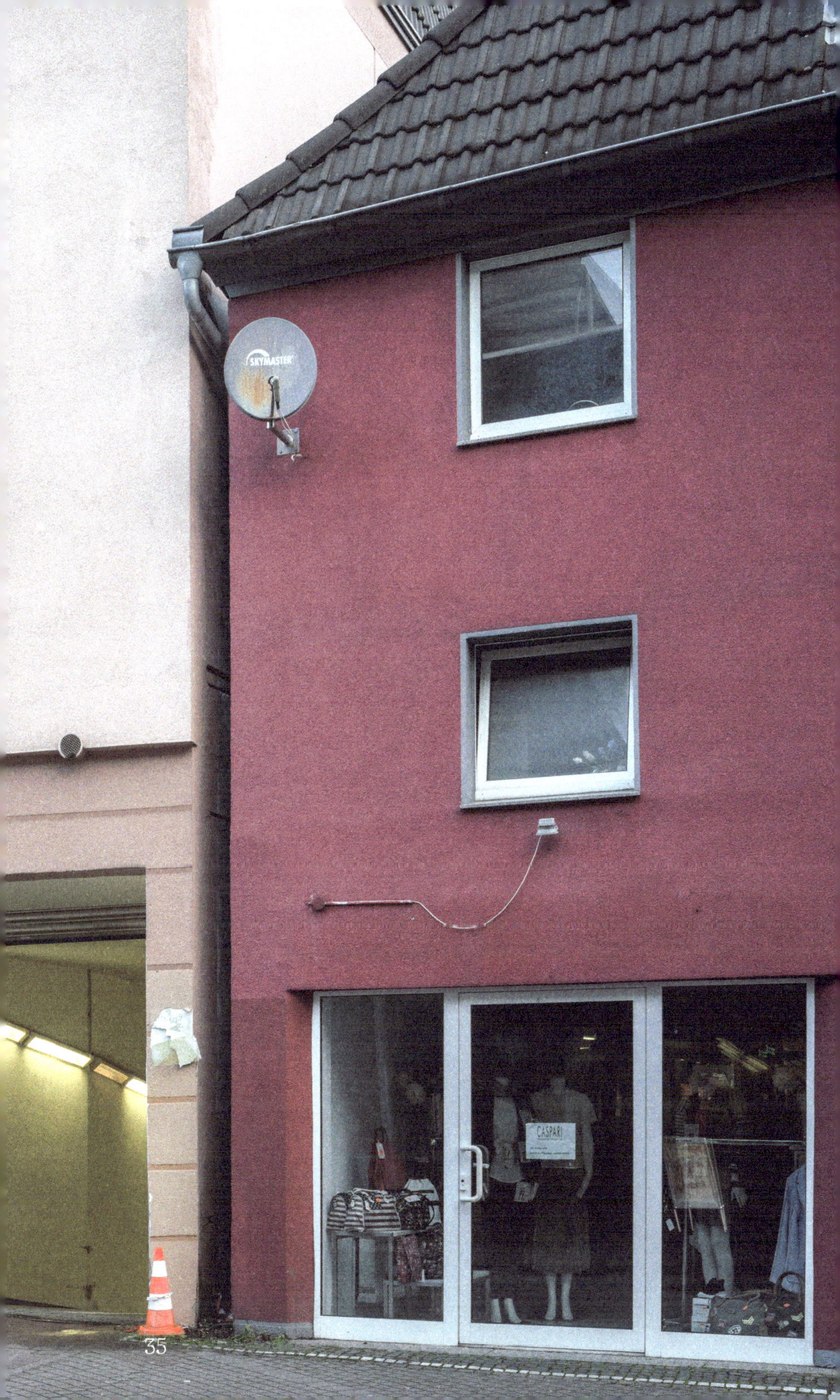
SKYMASTER
CASPARI

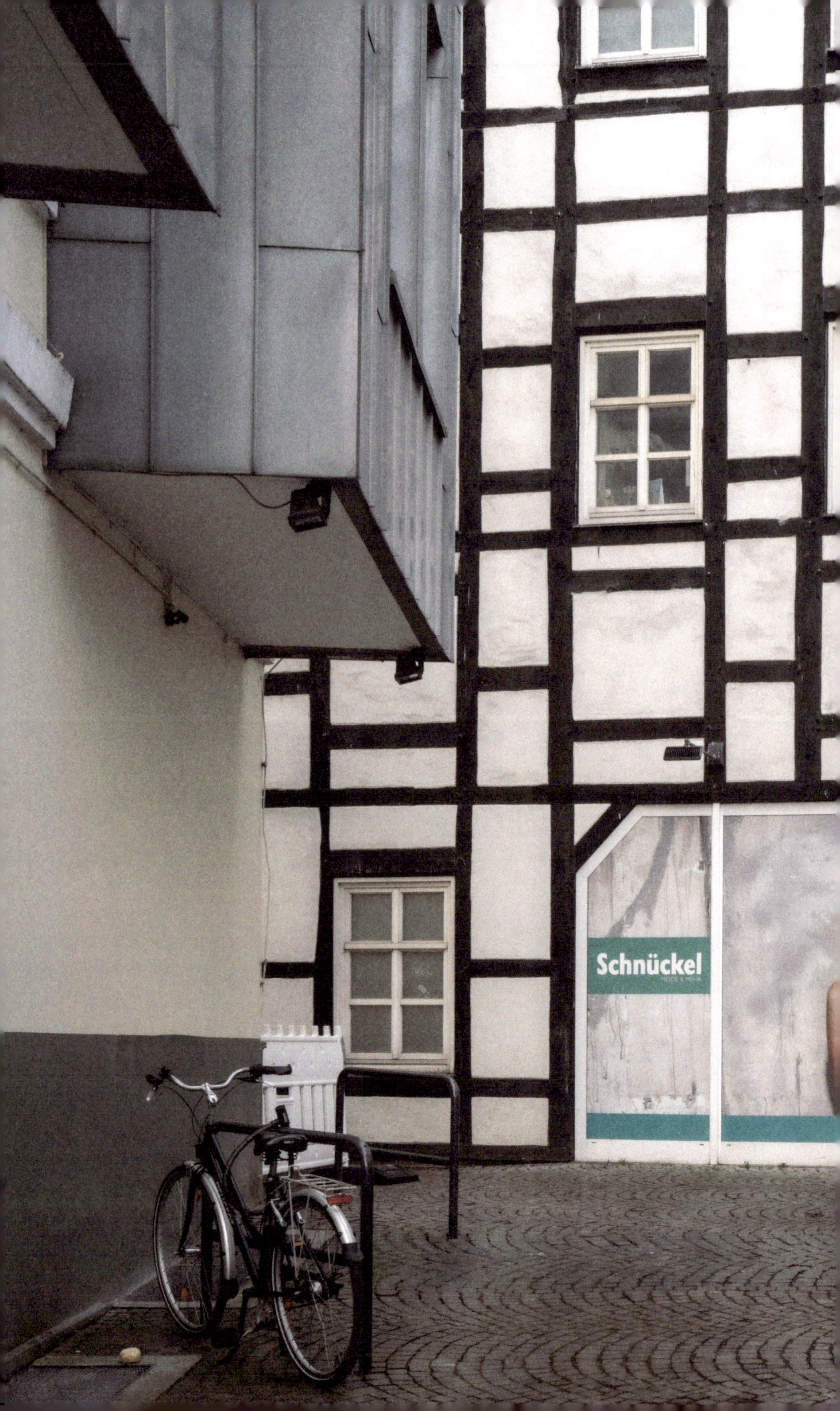
Schnückel

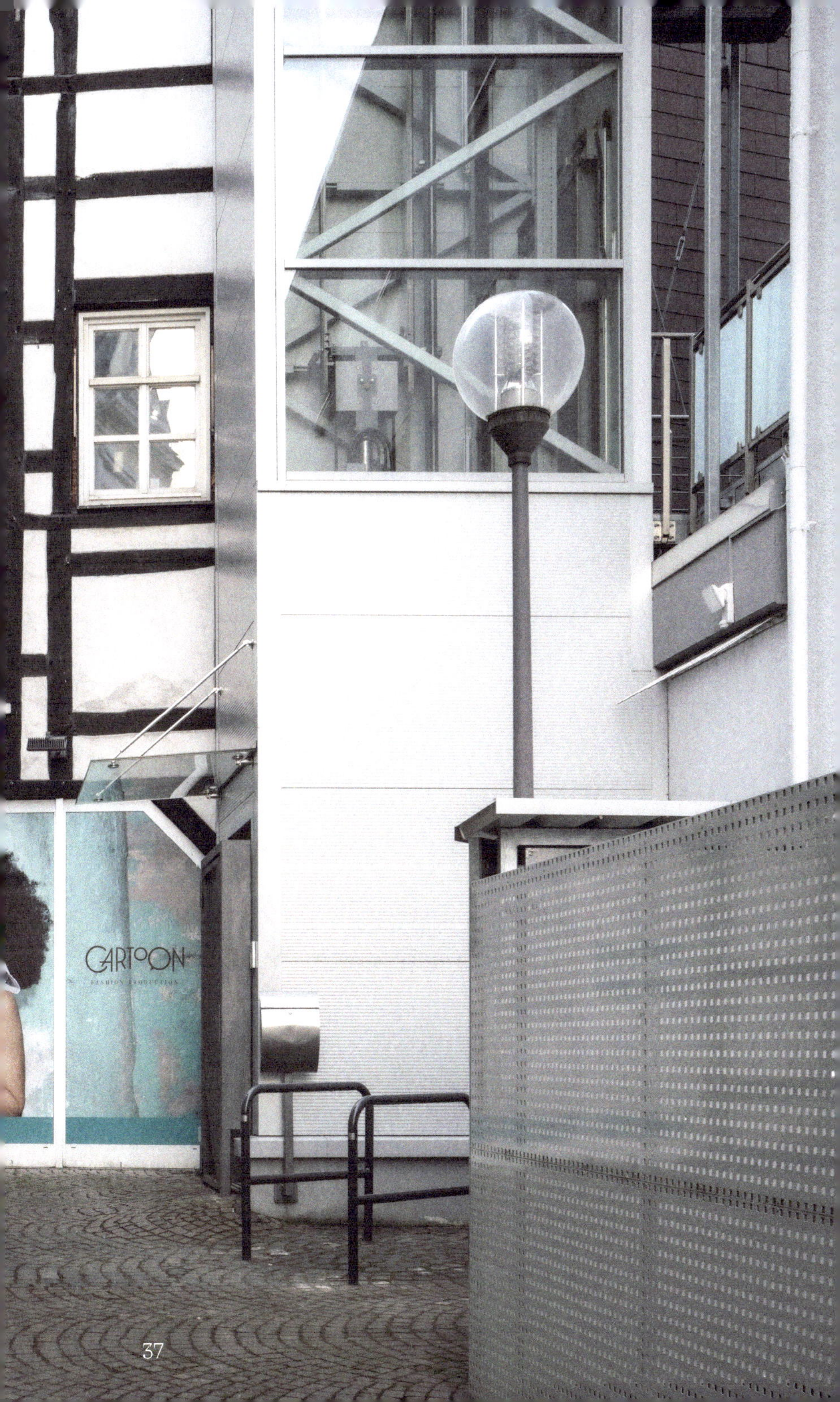
CARTOON
FASHION PRODUCTION

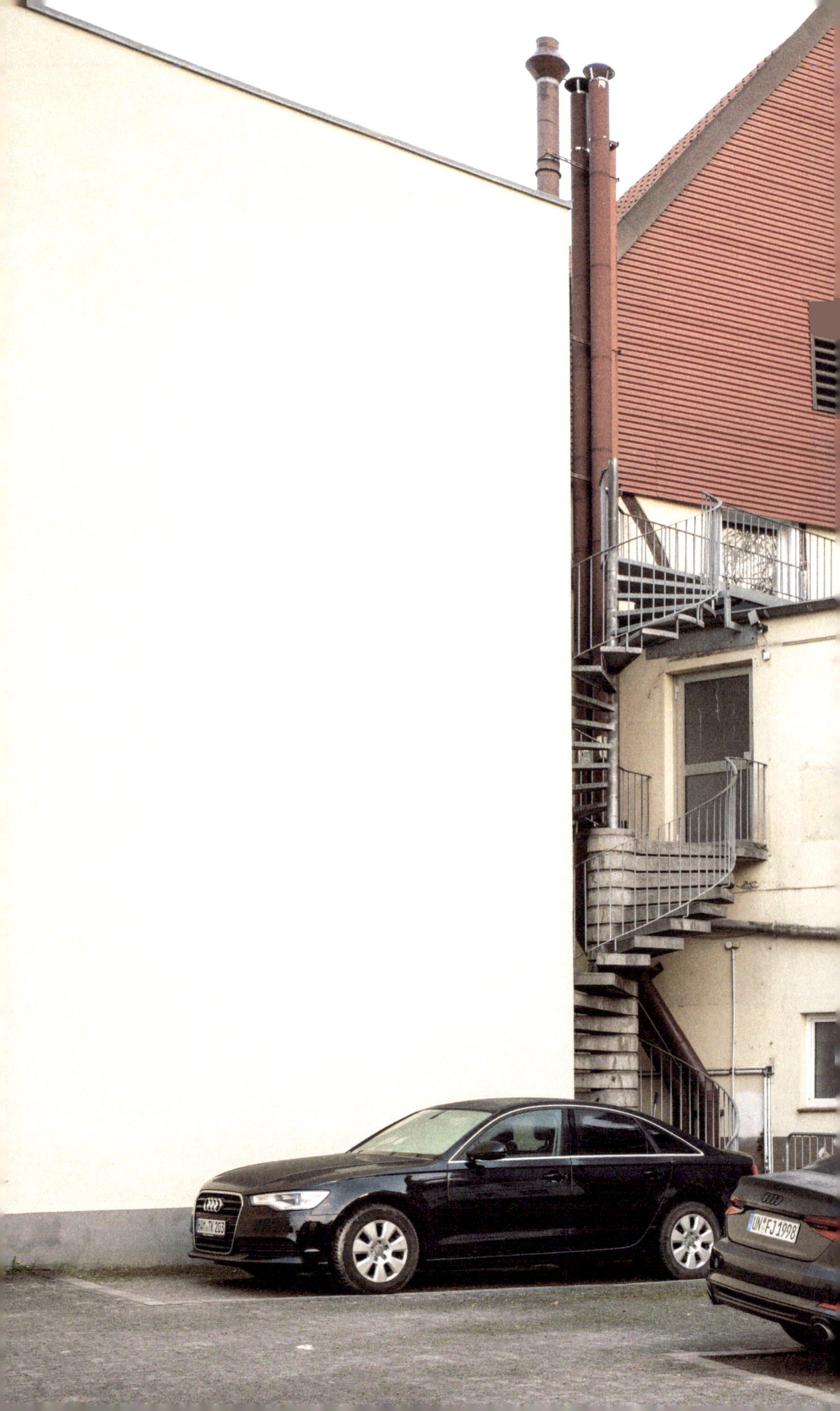
UN FJ 1998

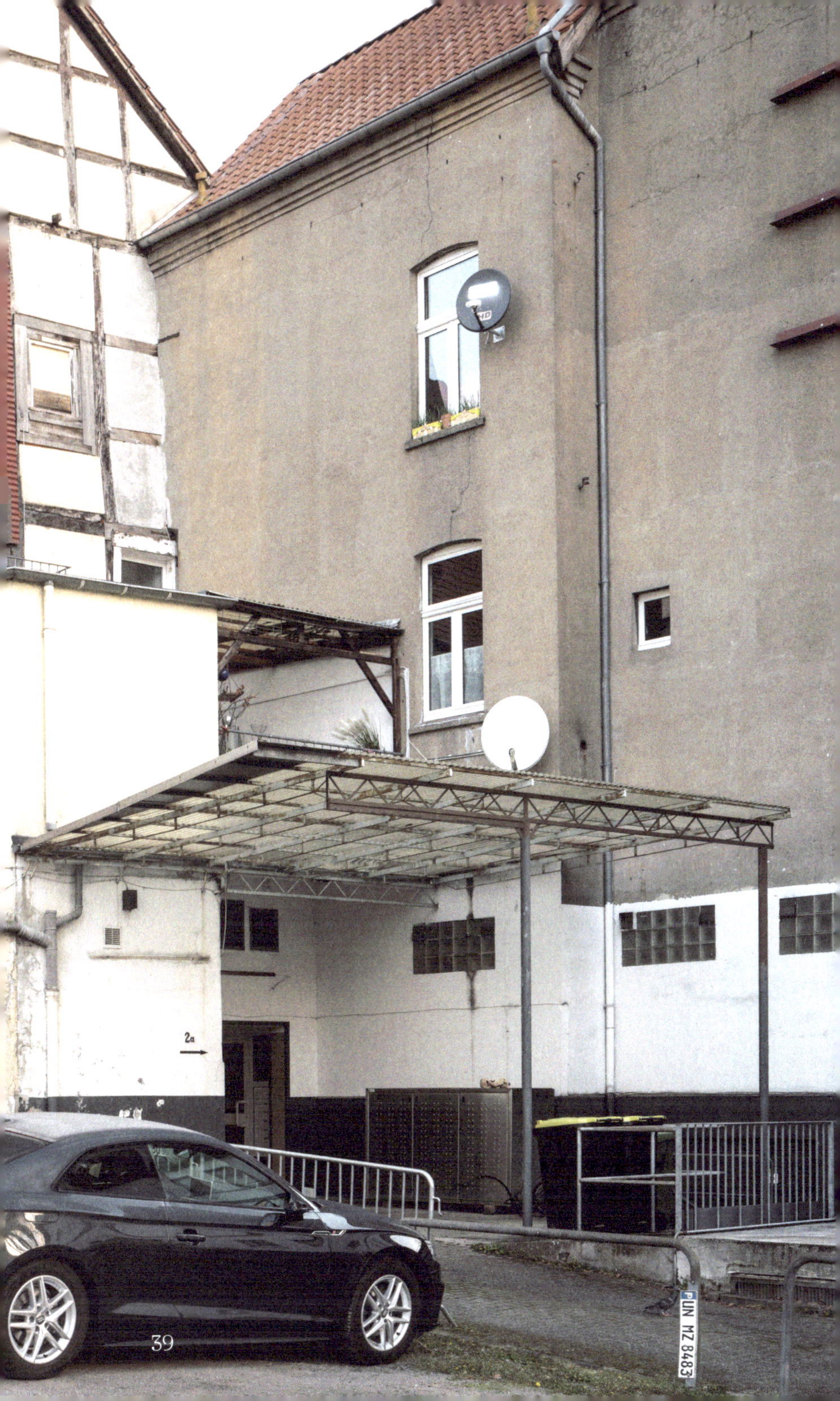
2a
PUN MZ 8483

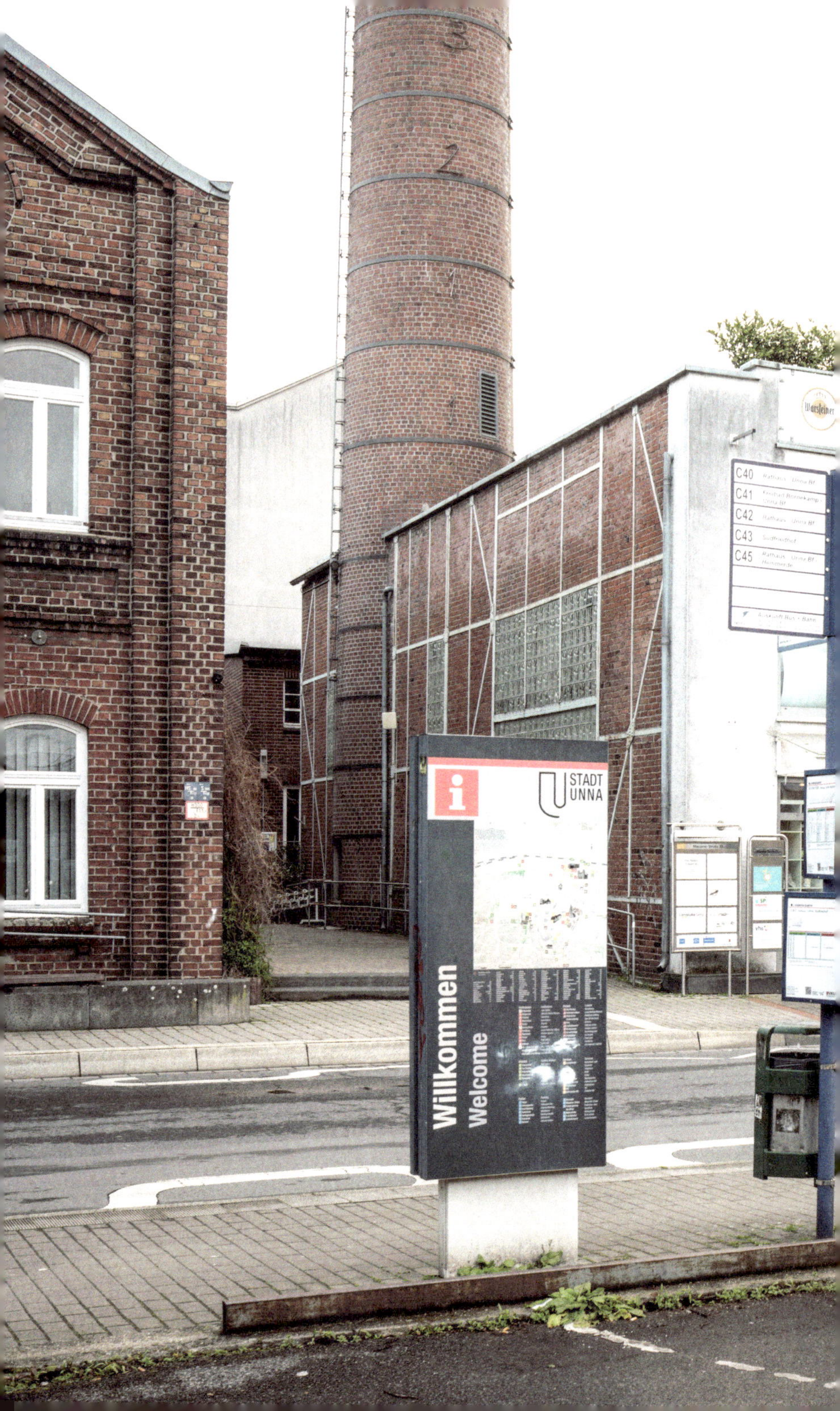
C40
C41
C42
C43
C45
i
STADT
UNNA
Willkommen
Welcome

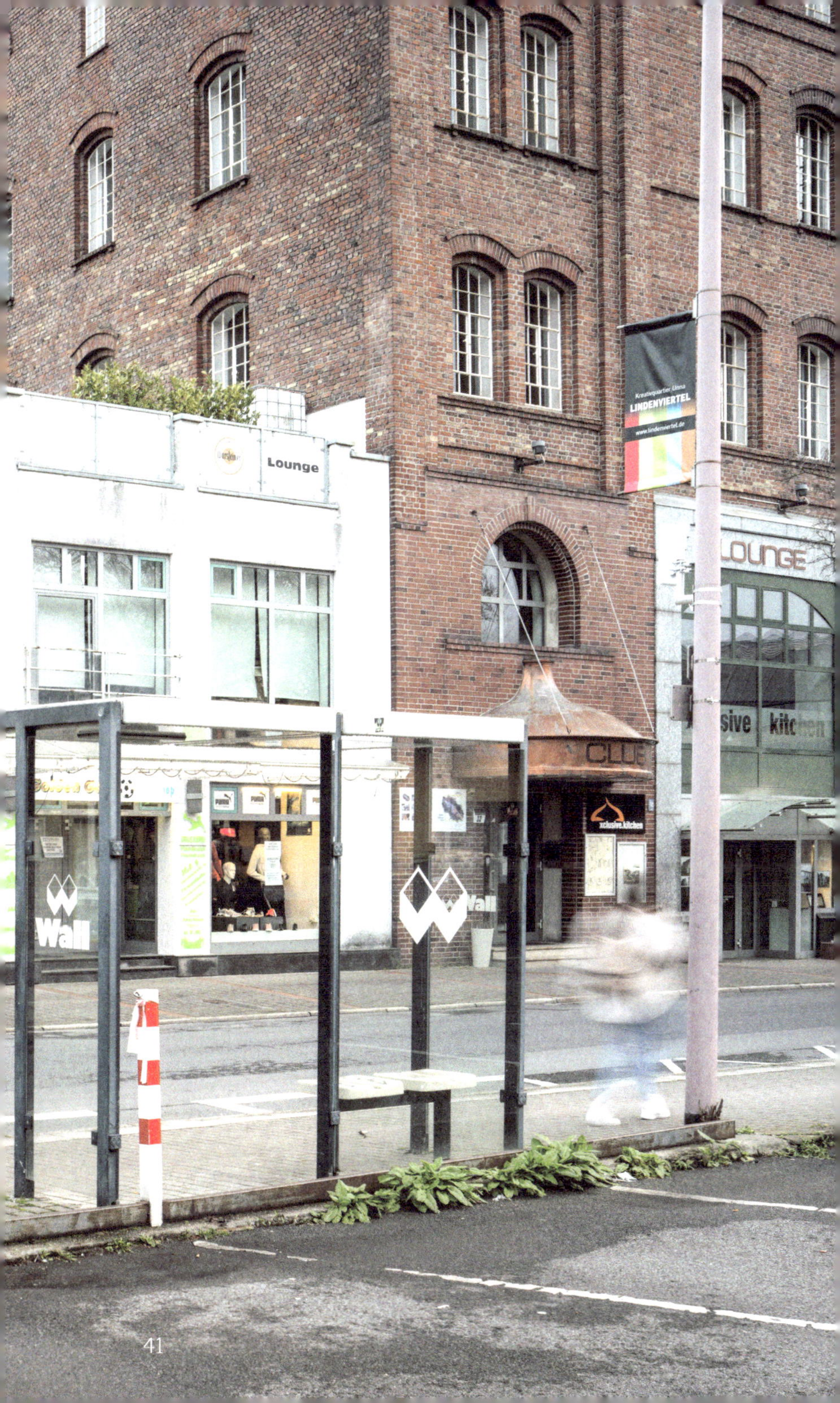
Lounge
LINDENVIERTEL
LOUNGE
CLUB
xclusive.kitchen
Wall
Wall

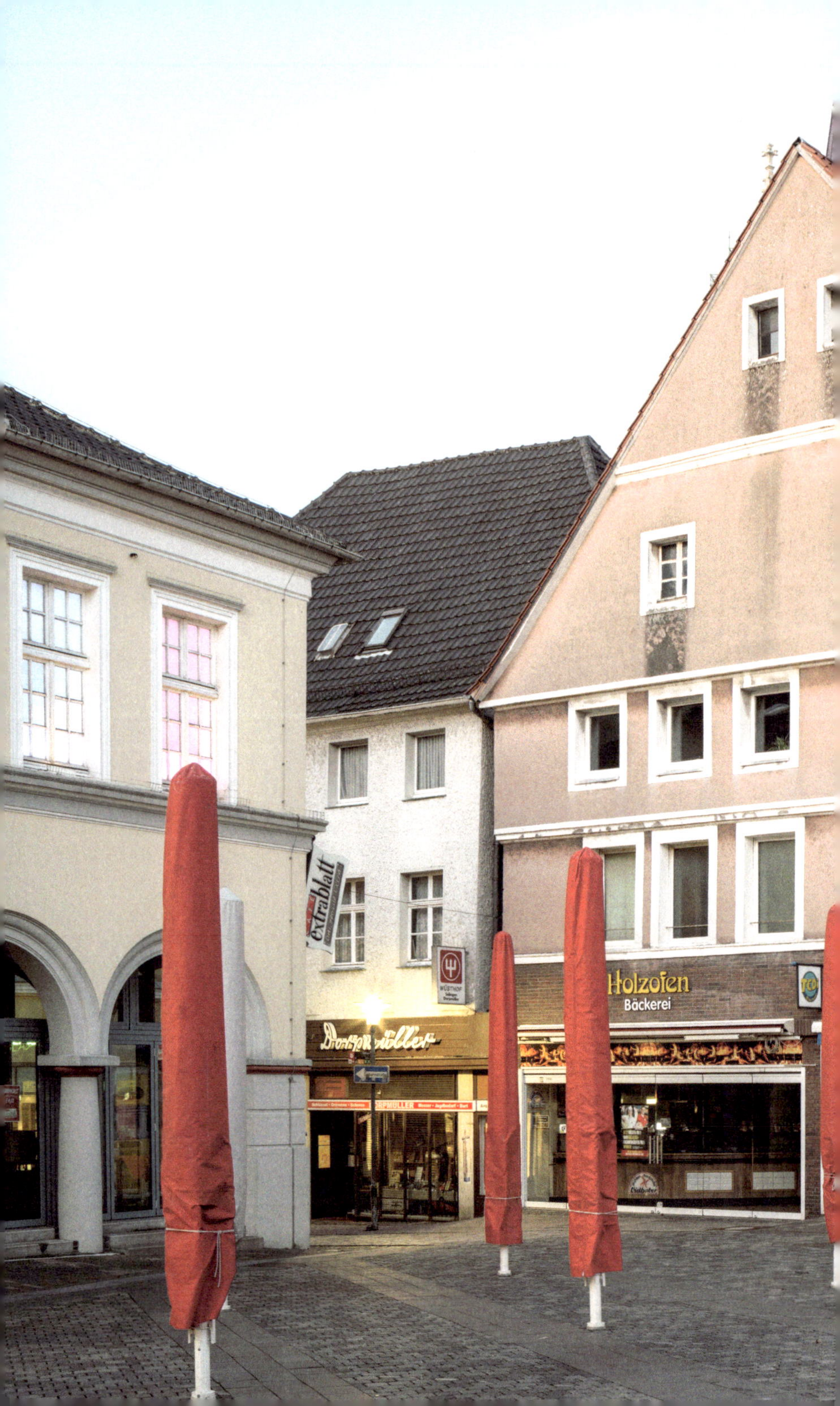
extrablatt
Holzofen
Bäckerei

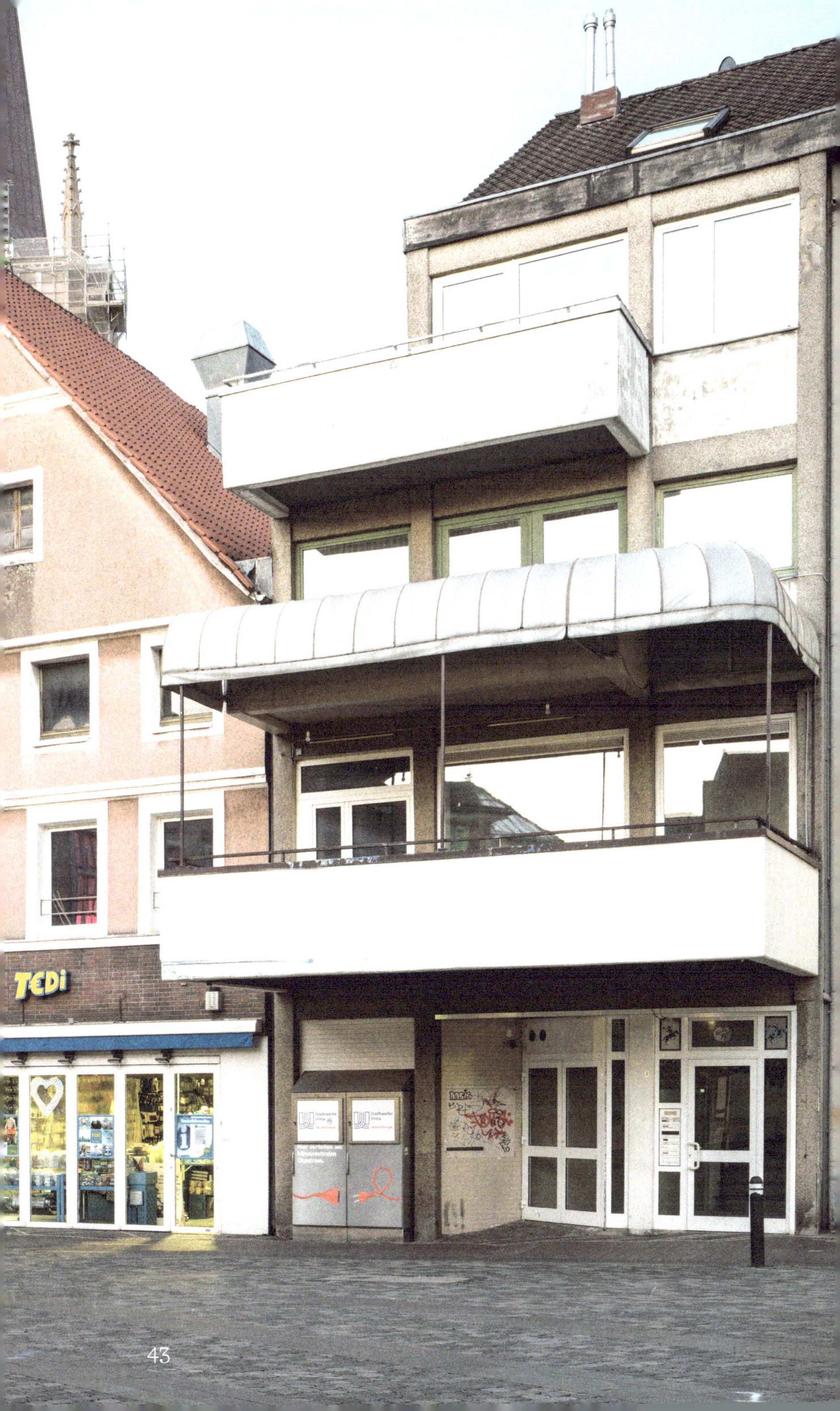
TEDi

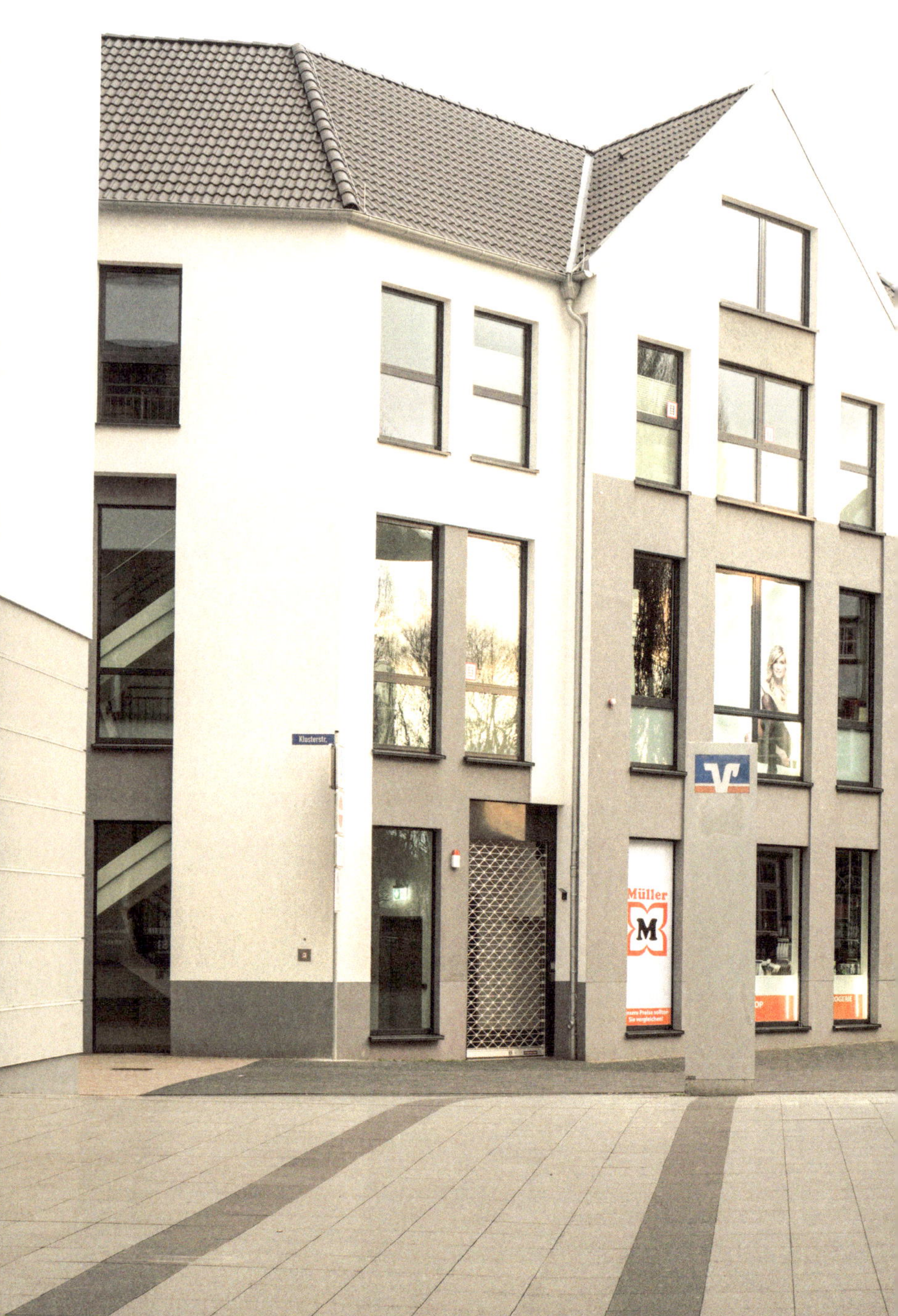
Klosterstr.
Müller
M

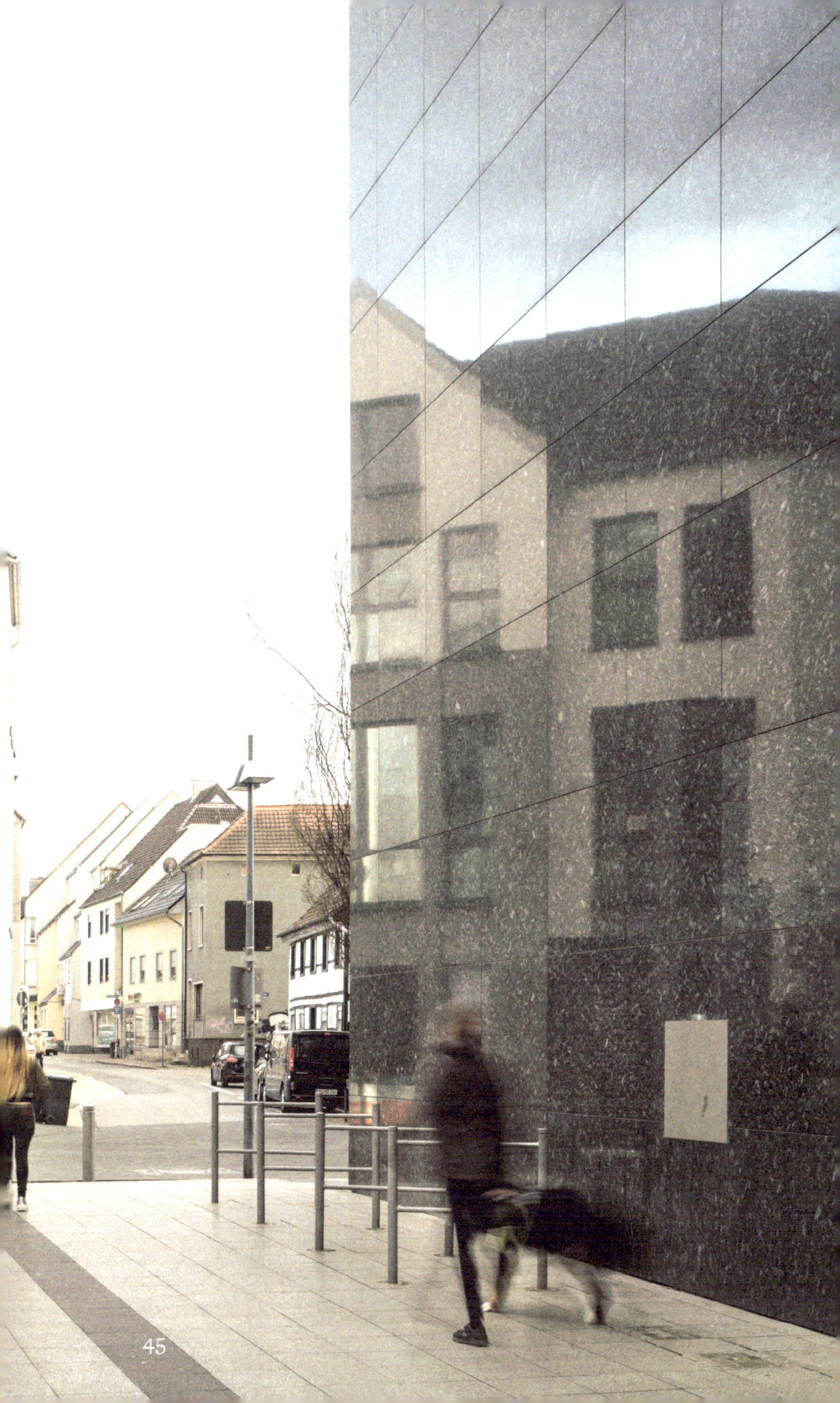

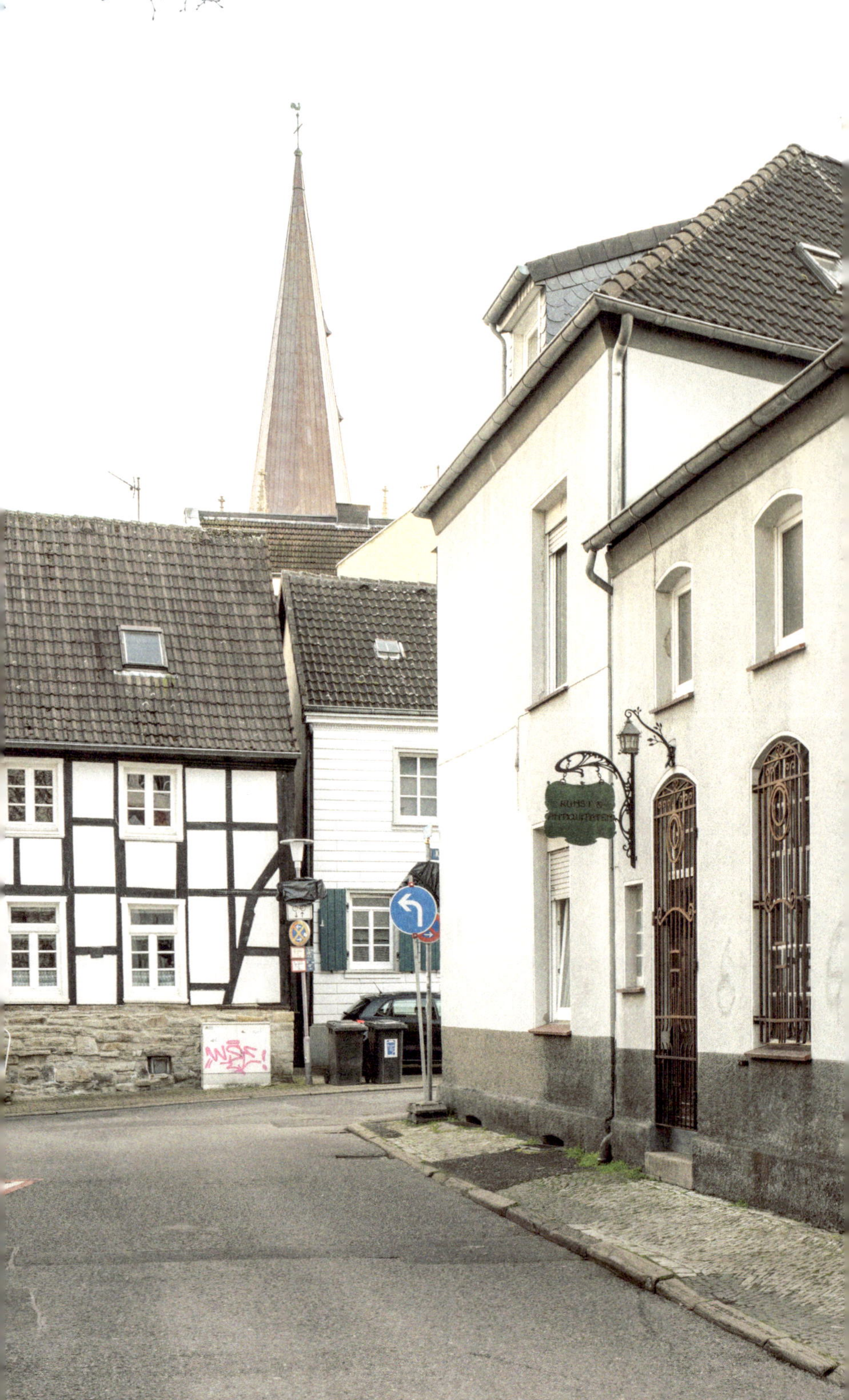
KUNST &

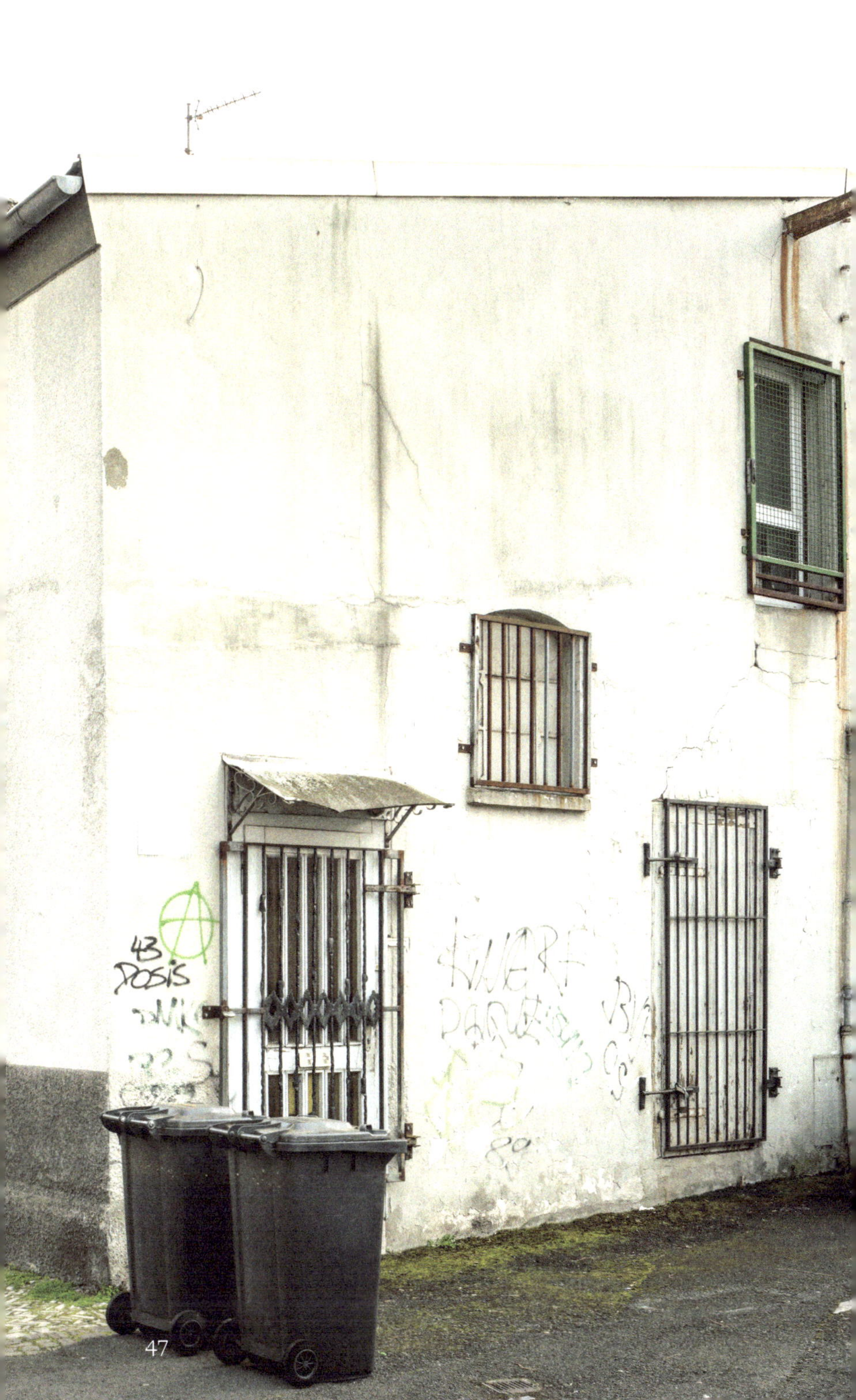
43
DOSIS

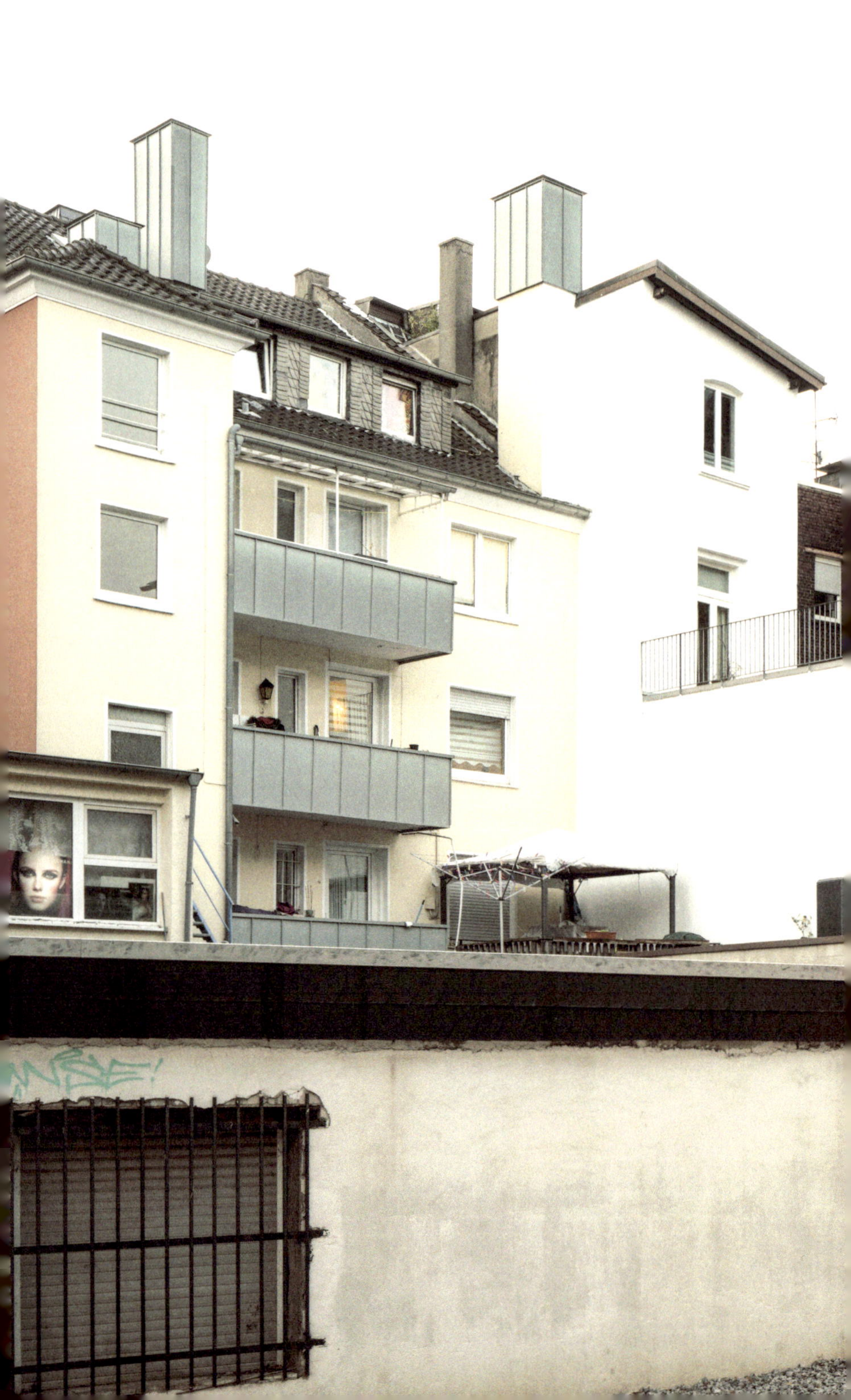

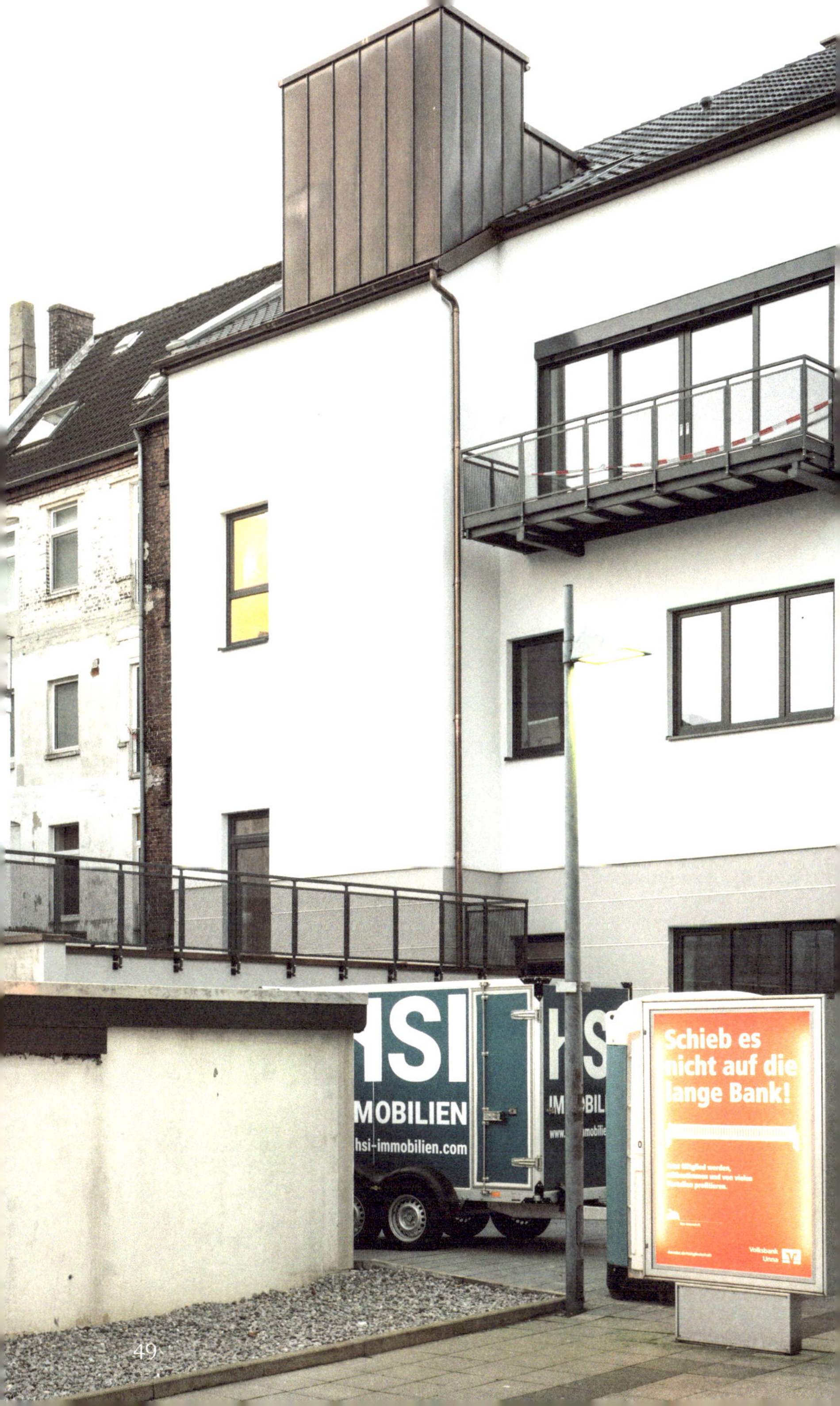
HSI
MOBILIEN
hsi-immobilien.com
Schieb es
icht auf die
ange Bank!
Volksbank
Unna

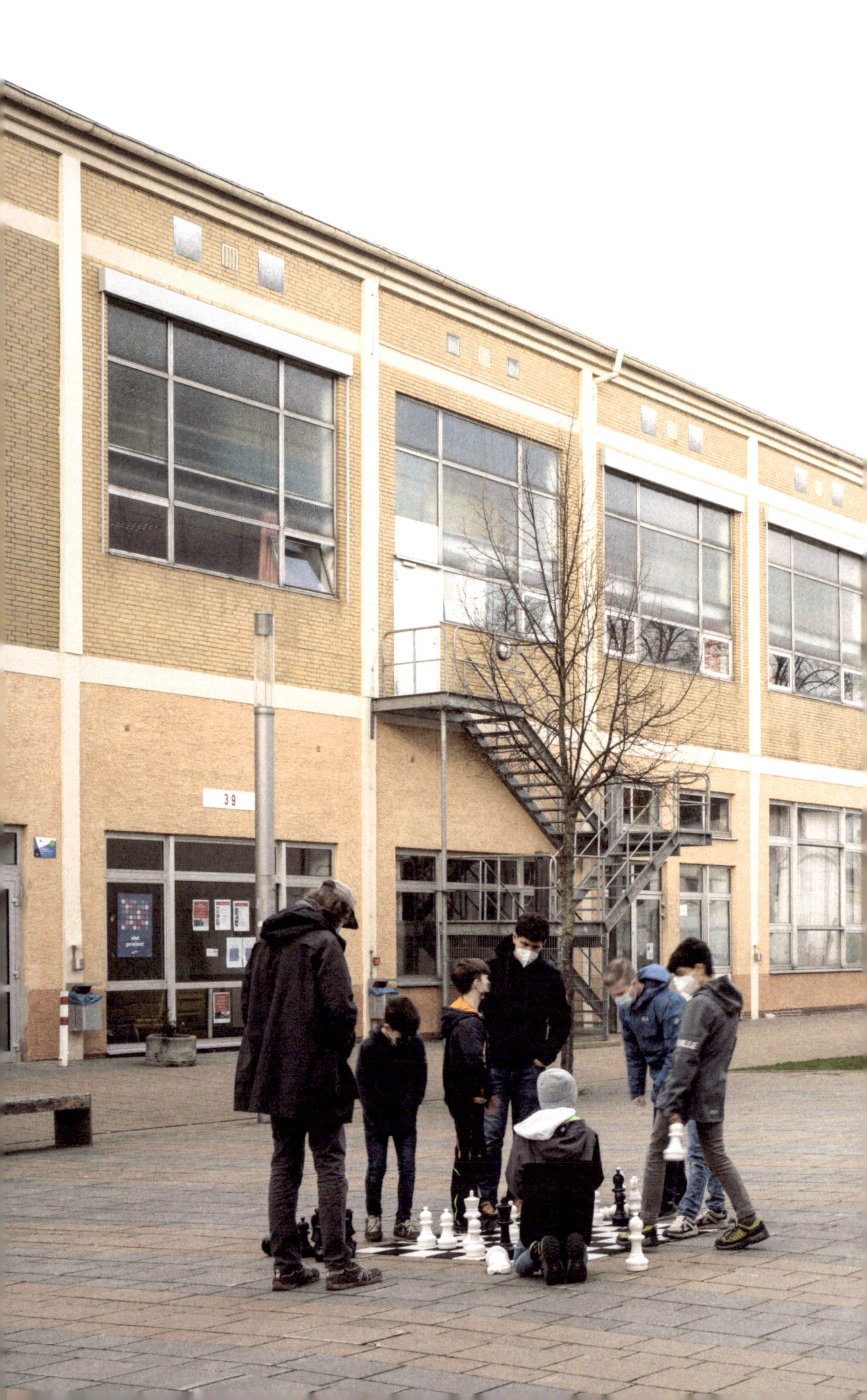
39

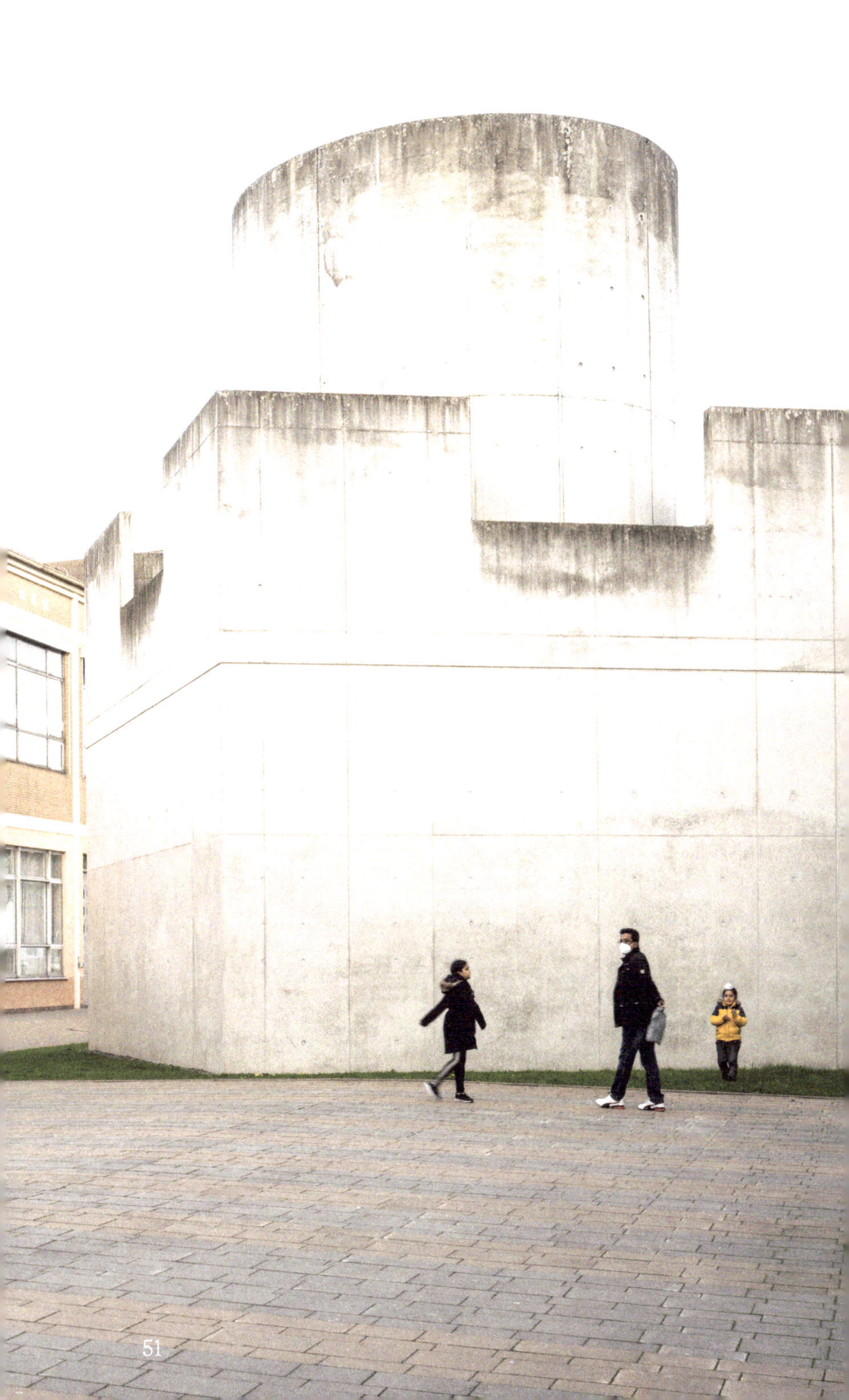

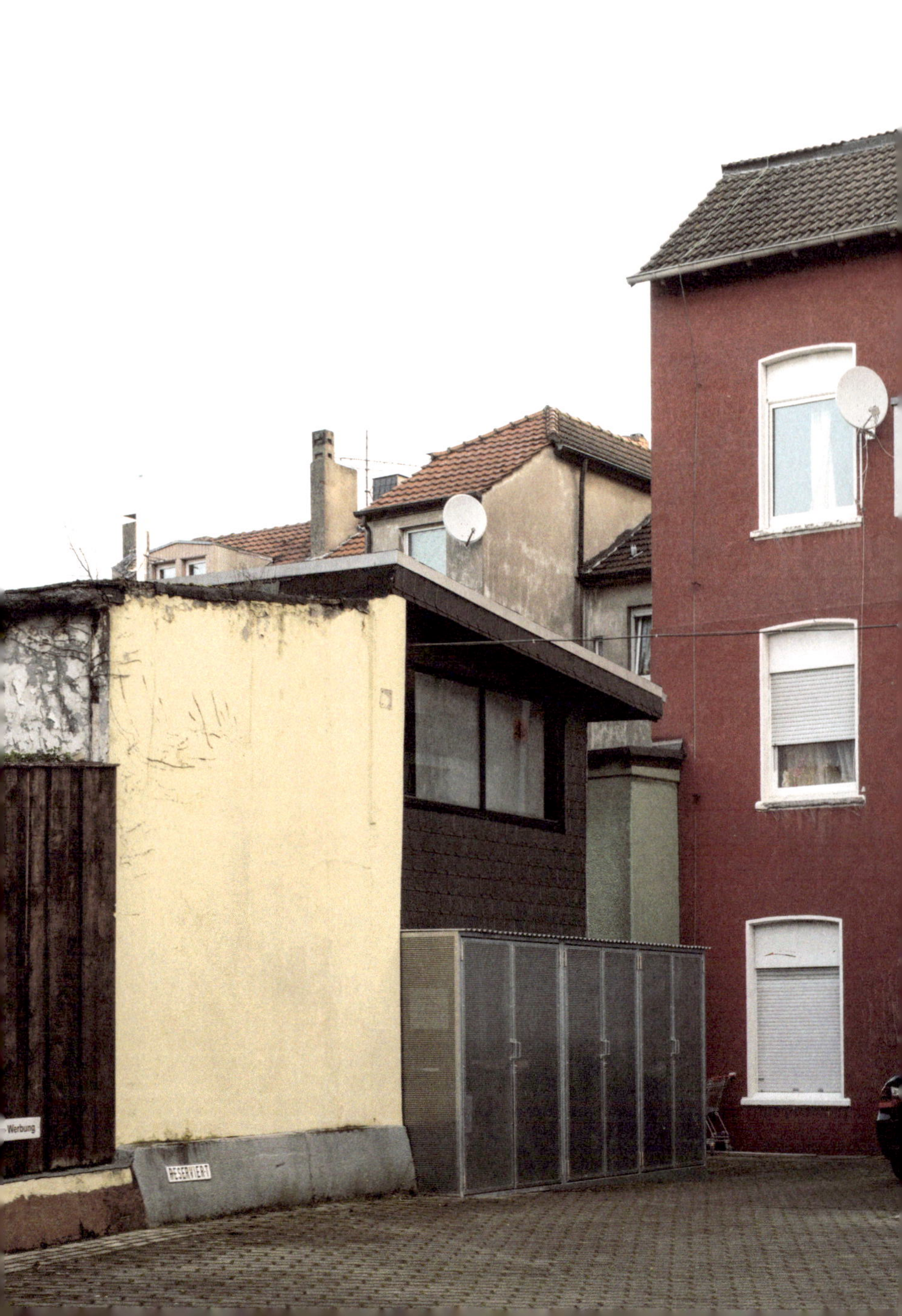
Werbung
RESERVIERT

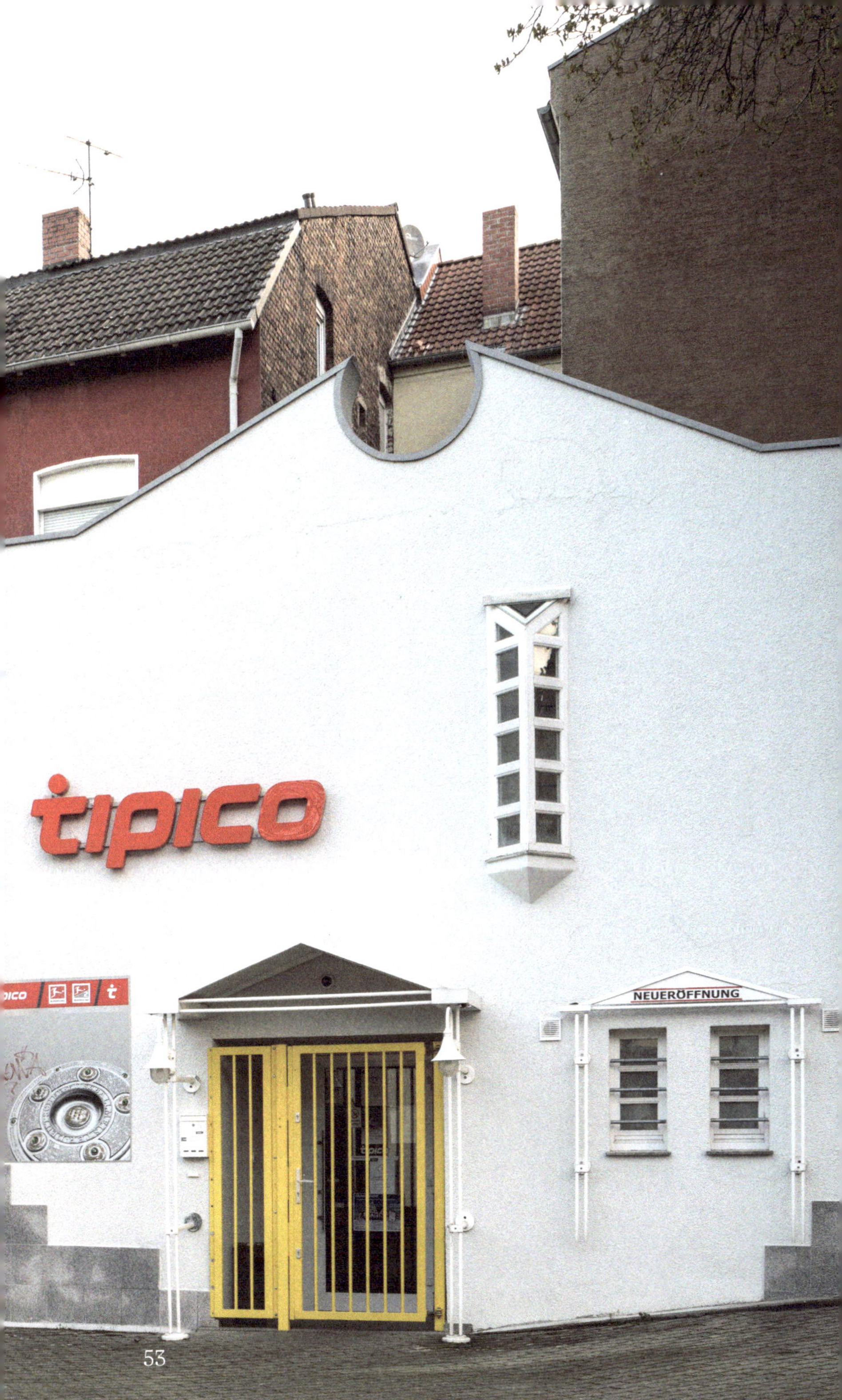
tipico
NEUERÖFFNUNG

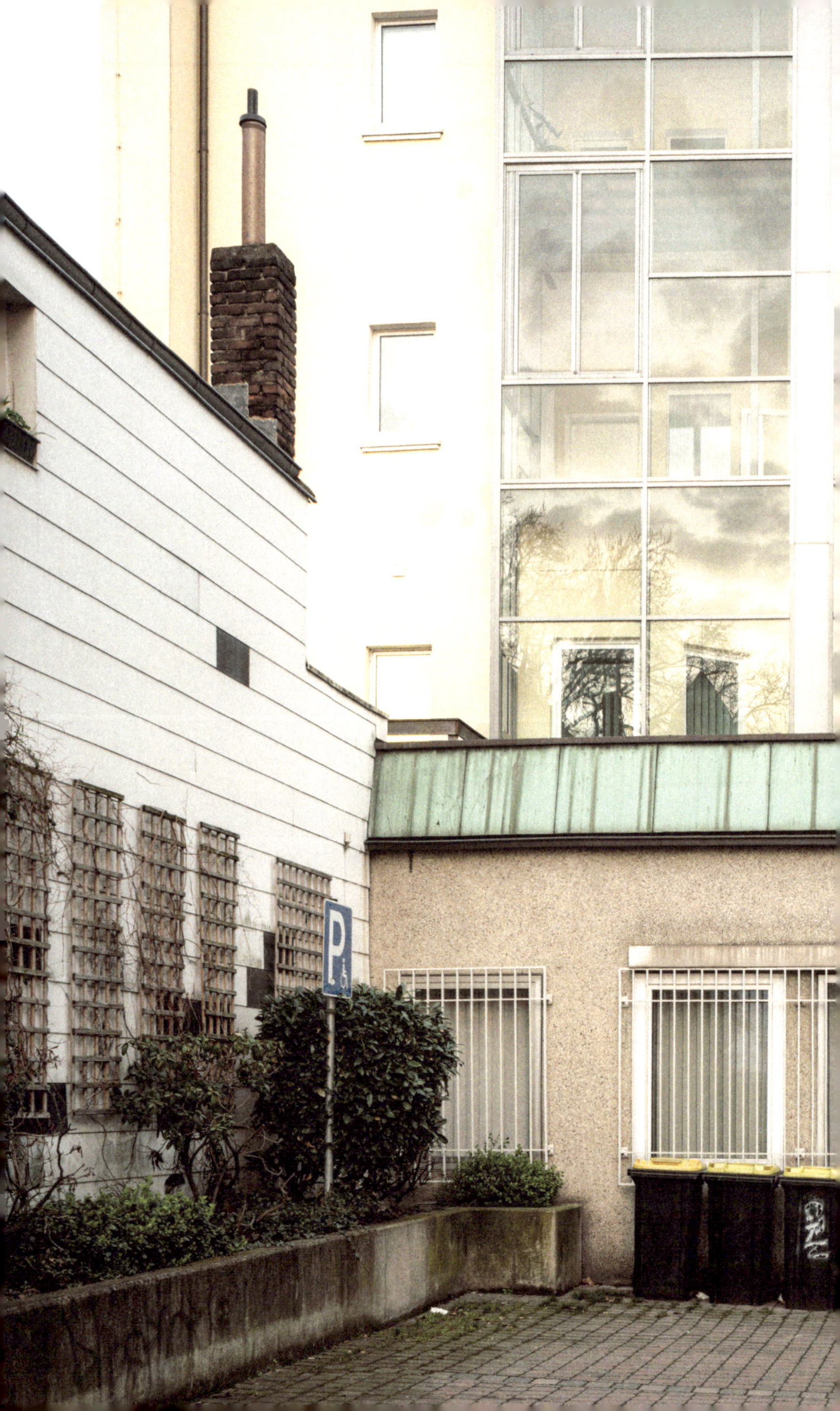
P

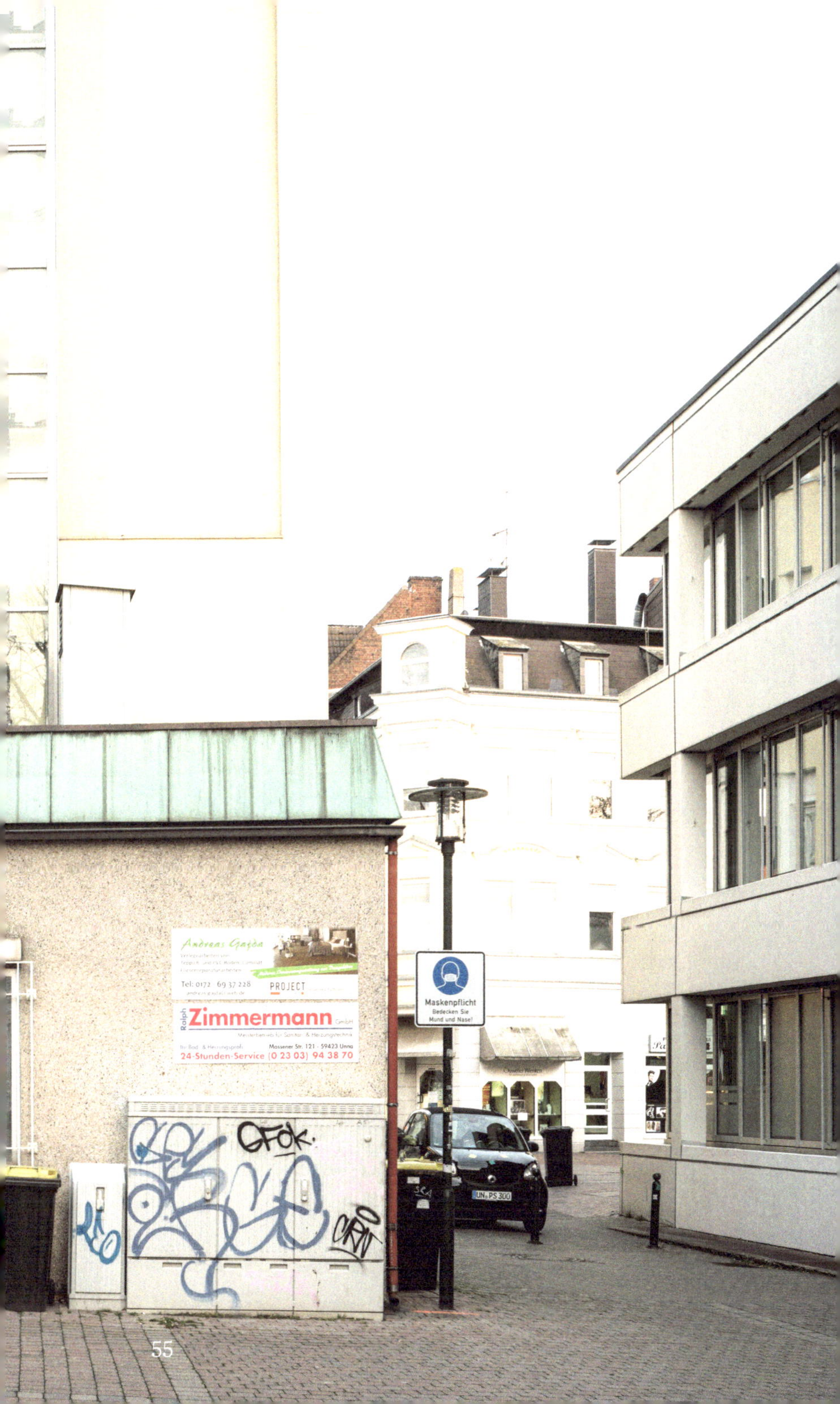
Andreas Gajda
Tel: 0172 69 37 228
PROJECT
Ralph Zimmermann GmbH
Massener Str. 121 · 59423 Unna
24-Stunden-Service (0 23 03) 94 38 70
Maskenpflicht
Bedecken Sie
Mund und Nase!
UN PS 300

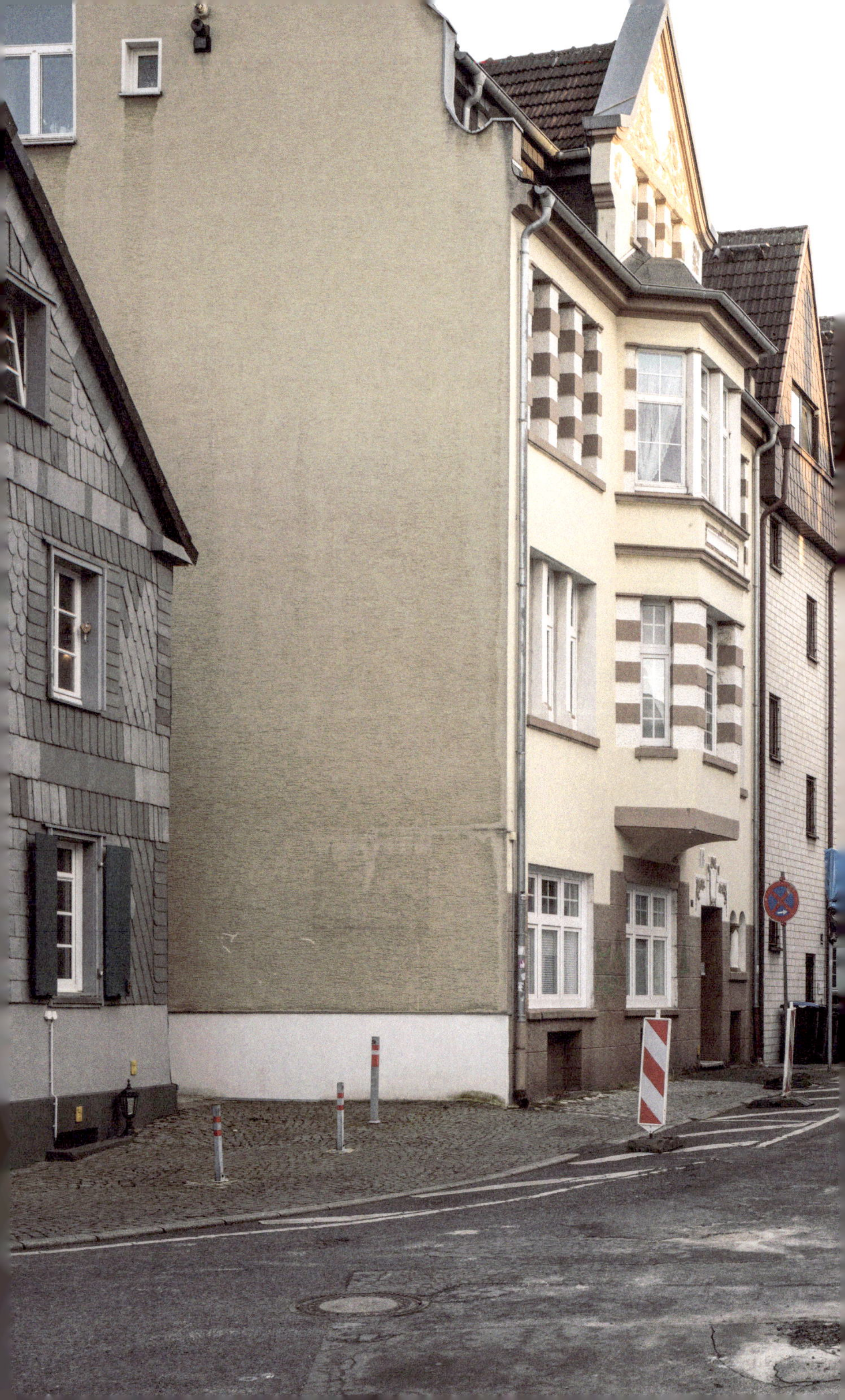

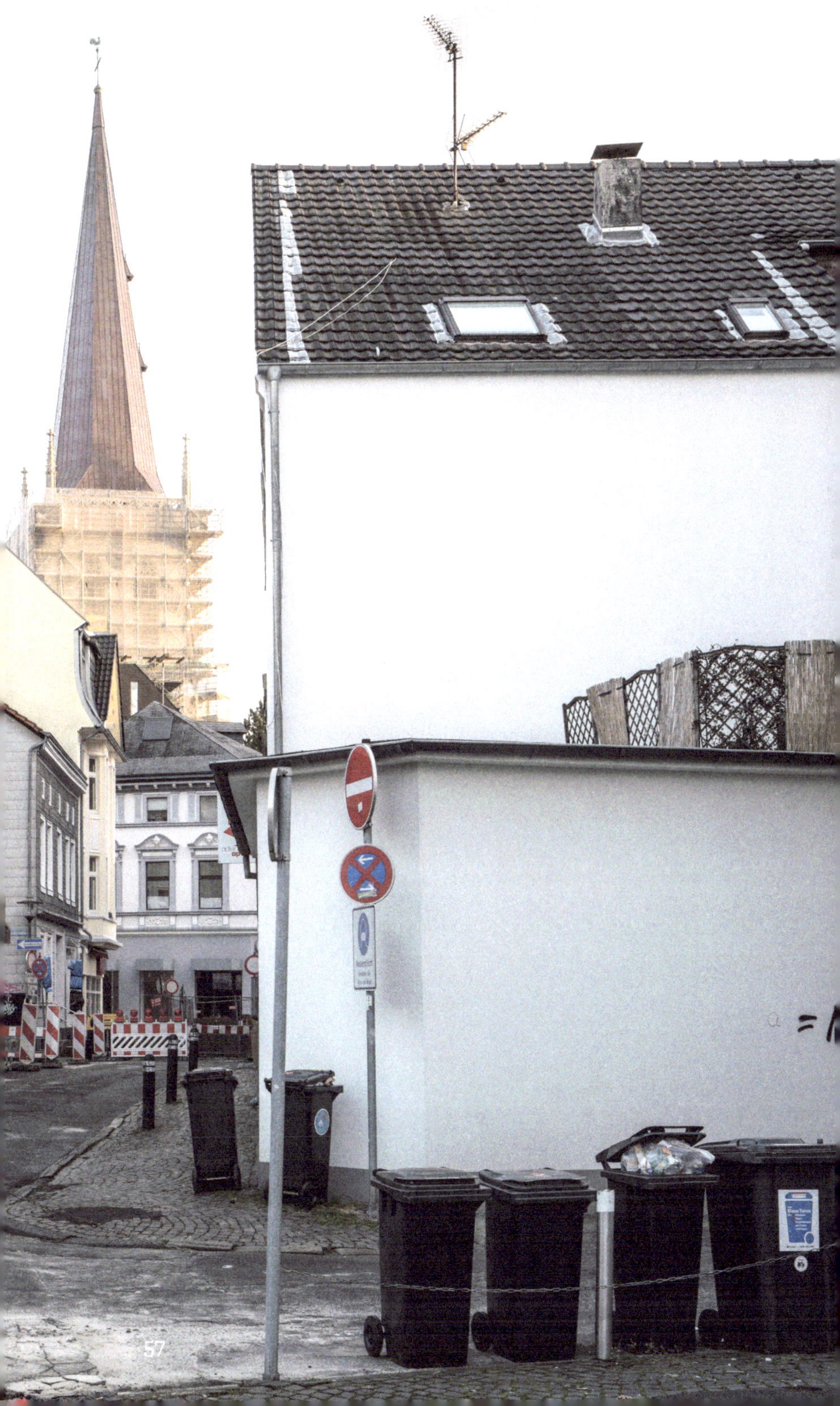

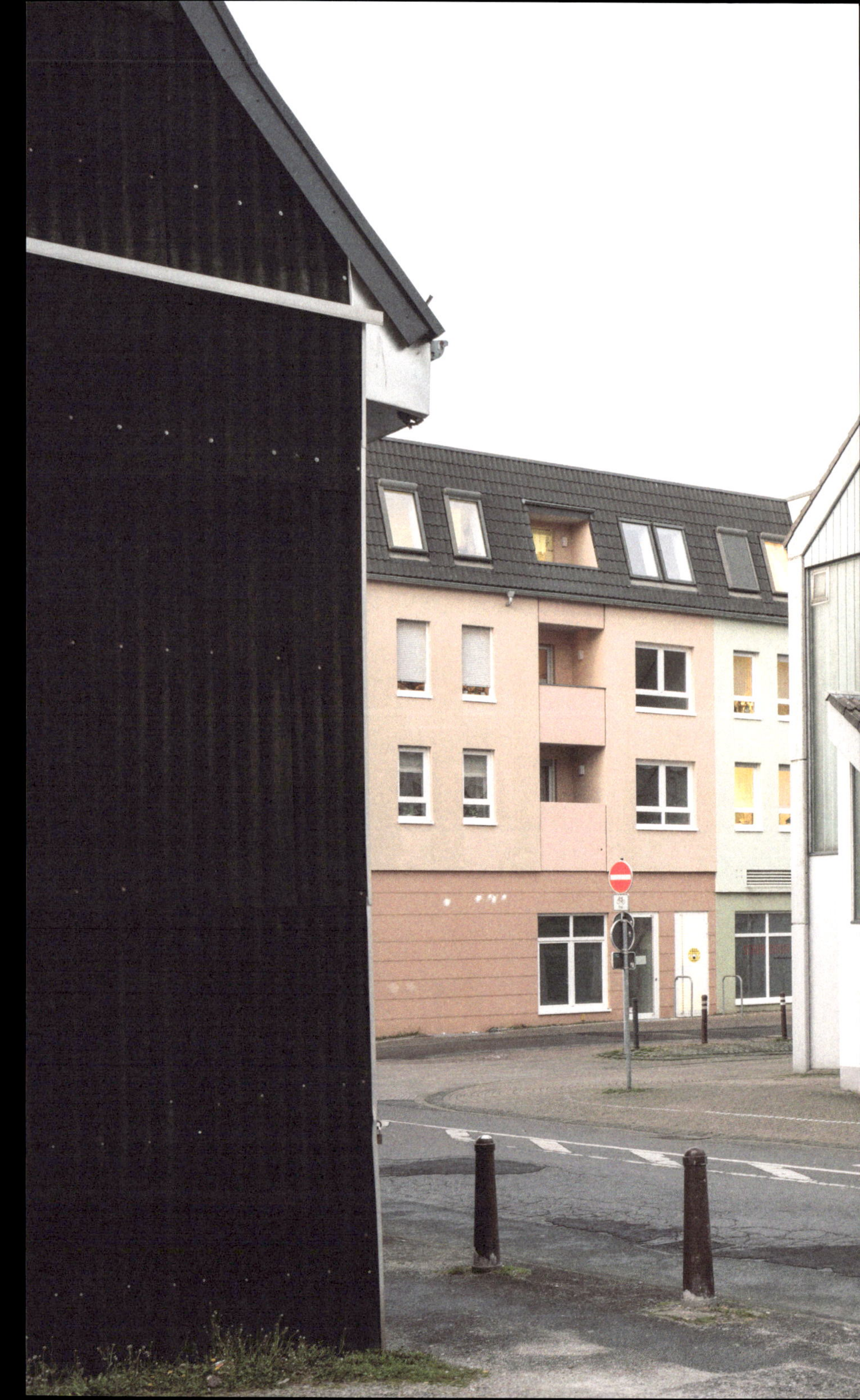

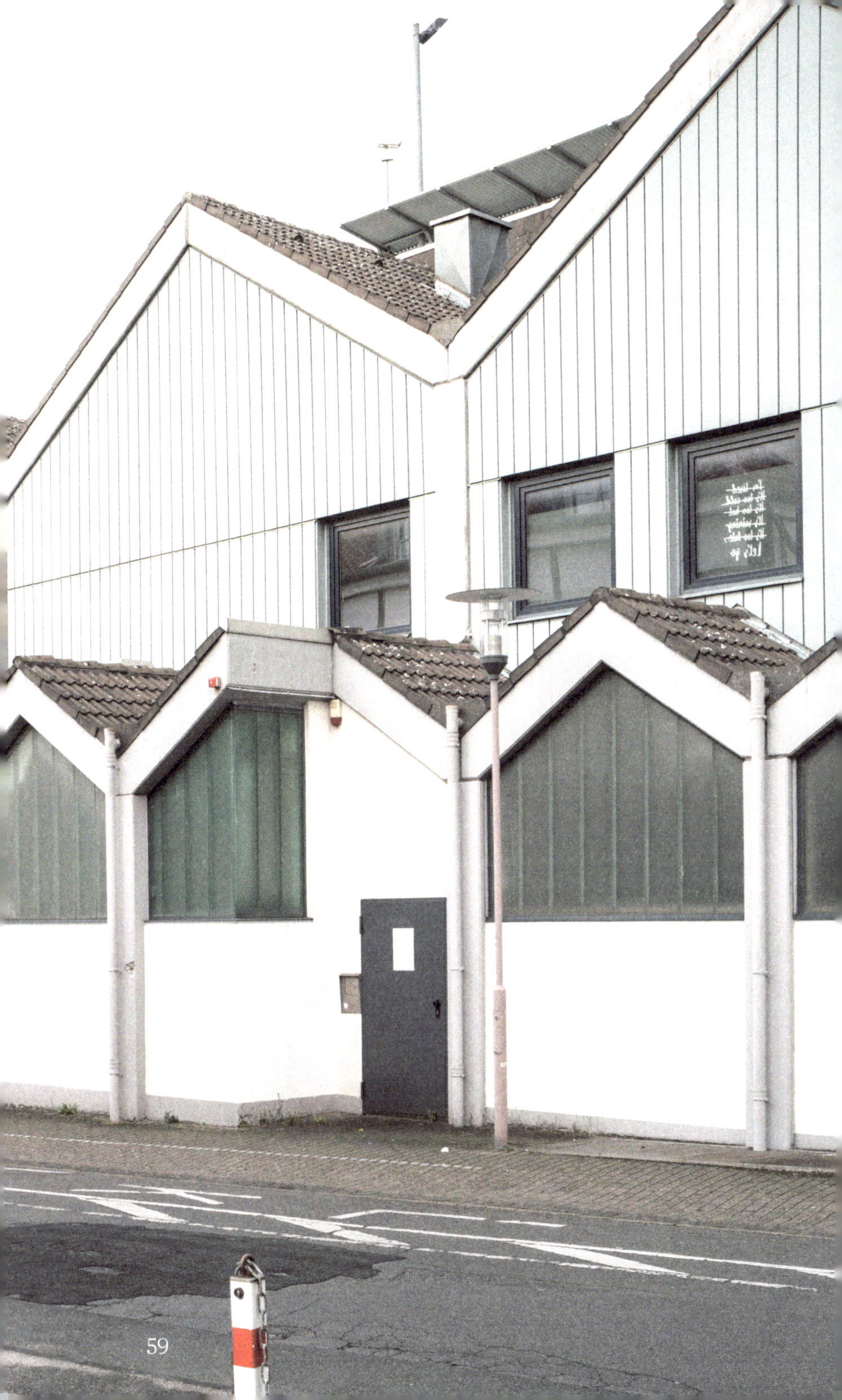

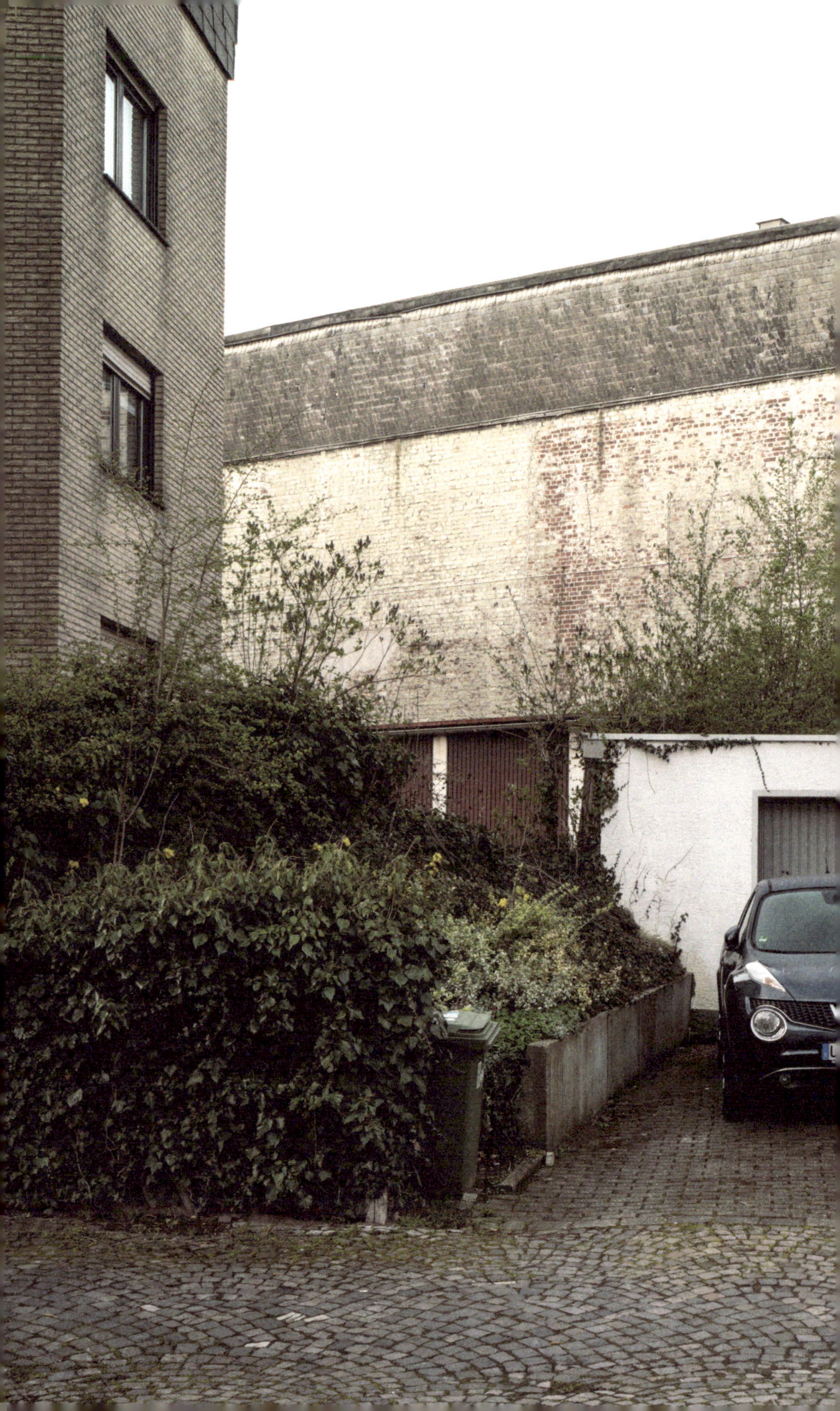

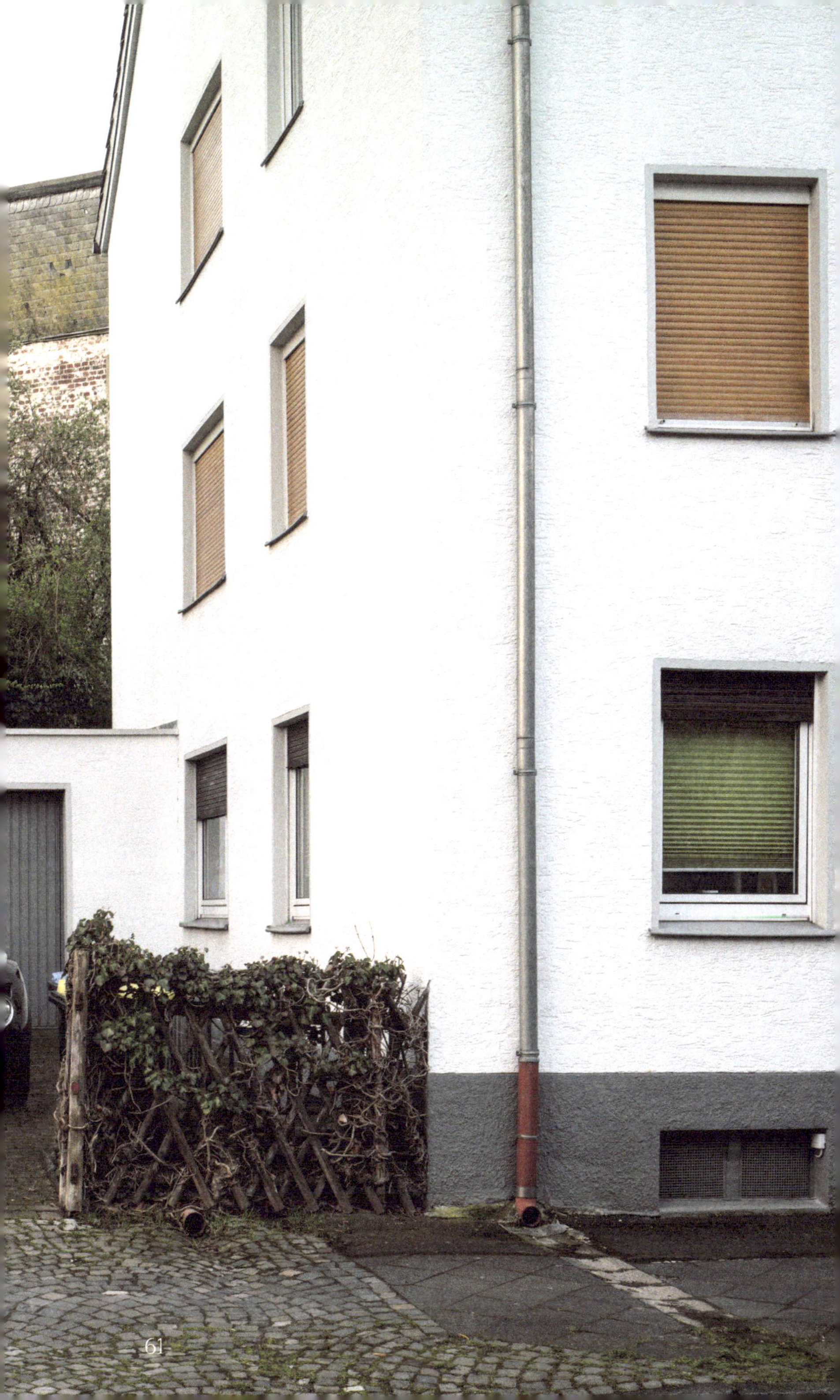

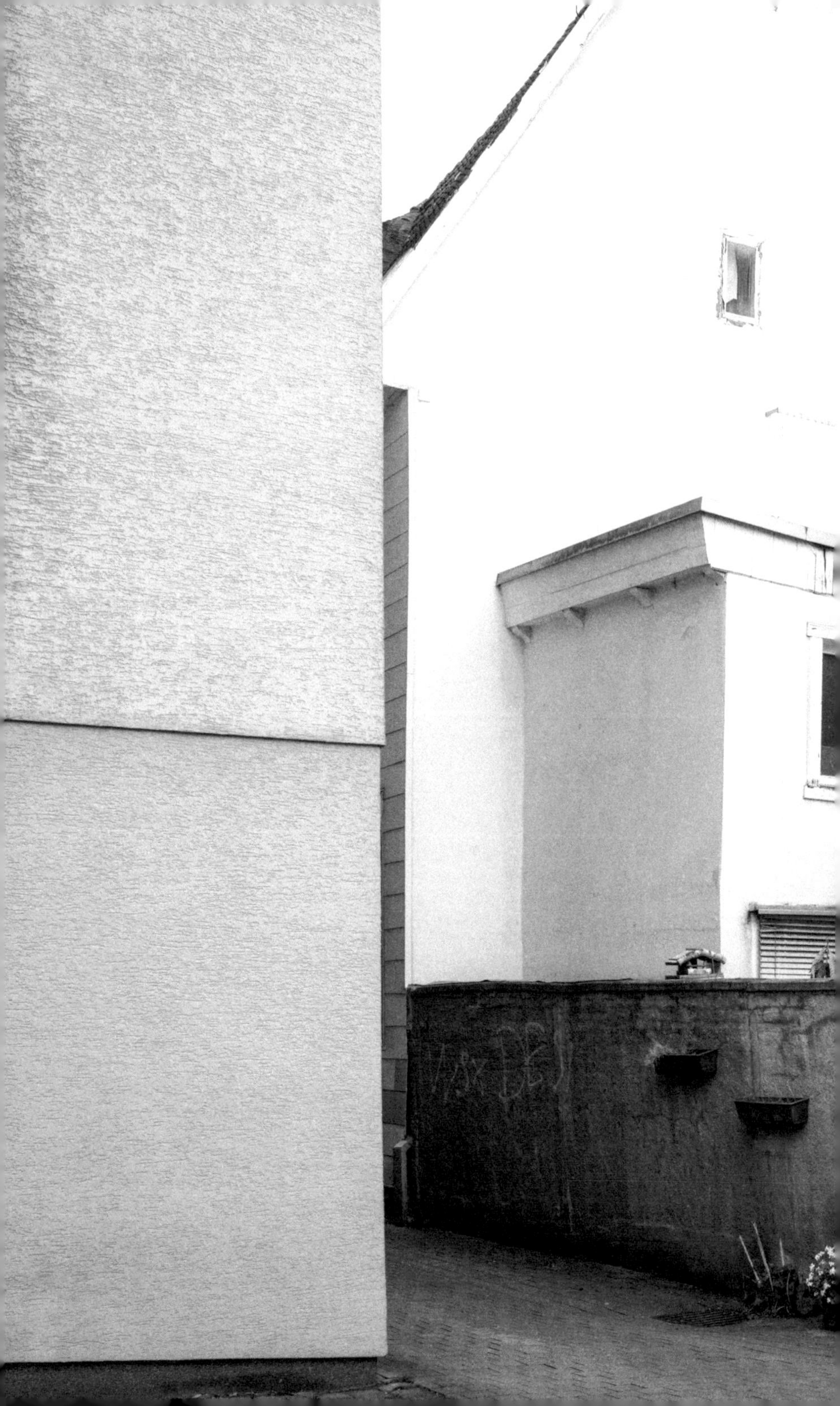

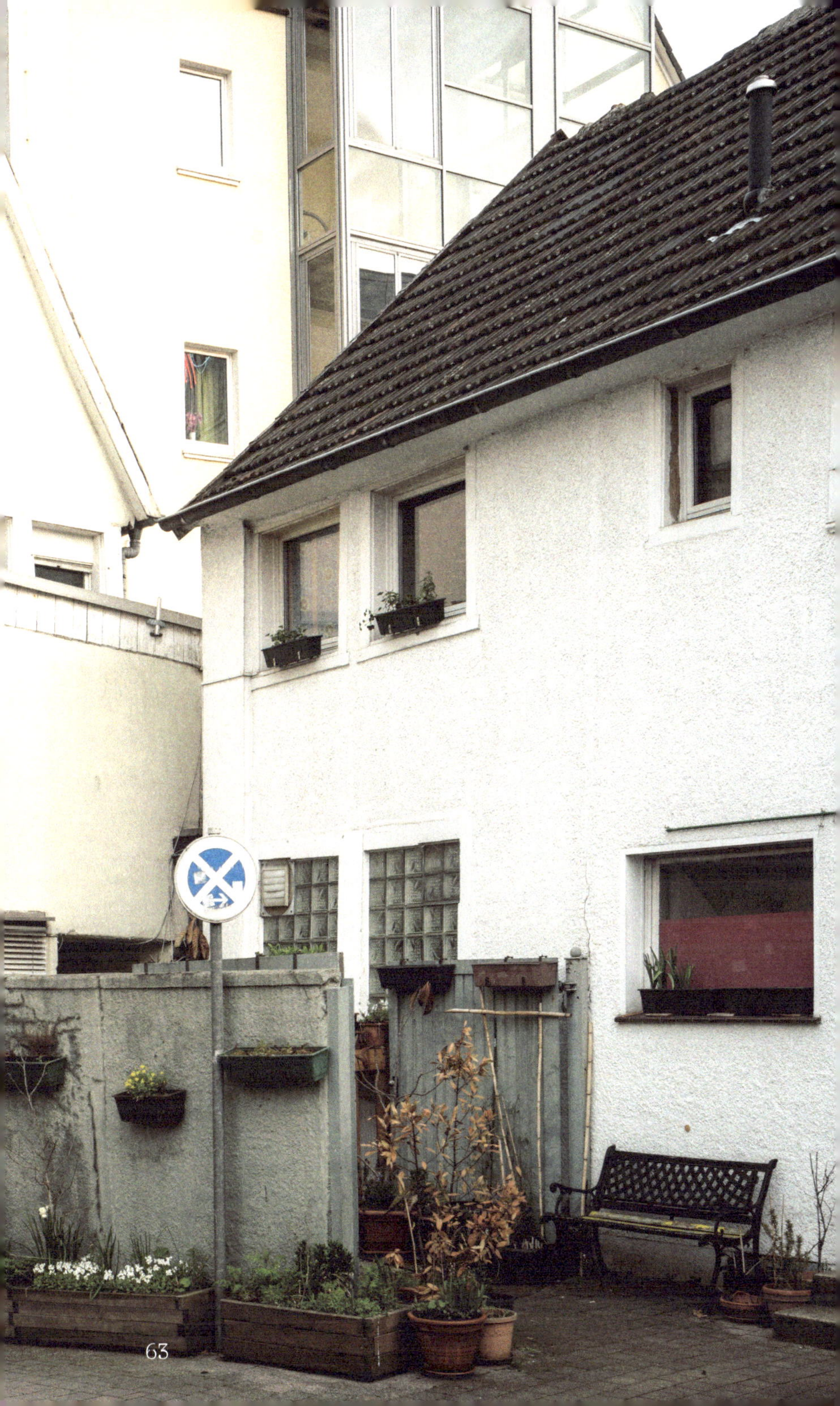

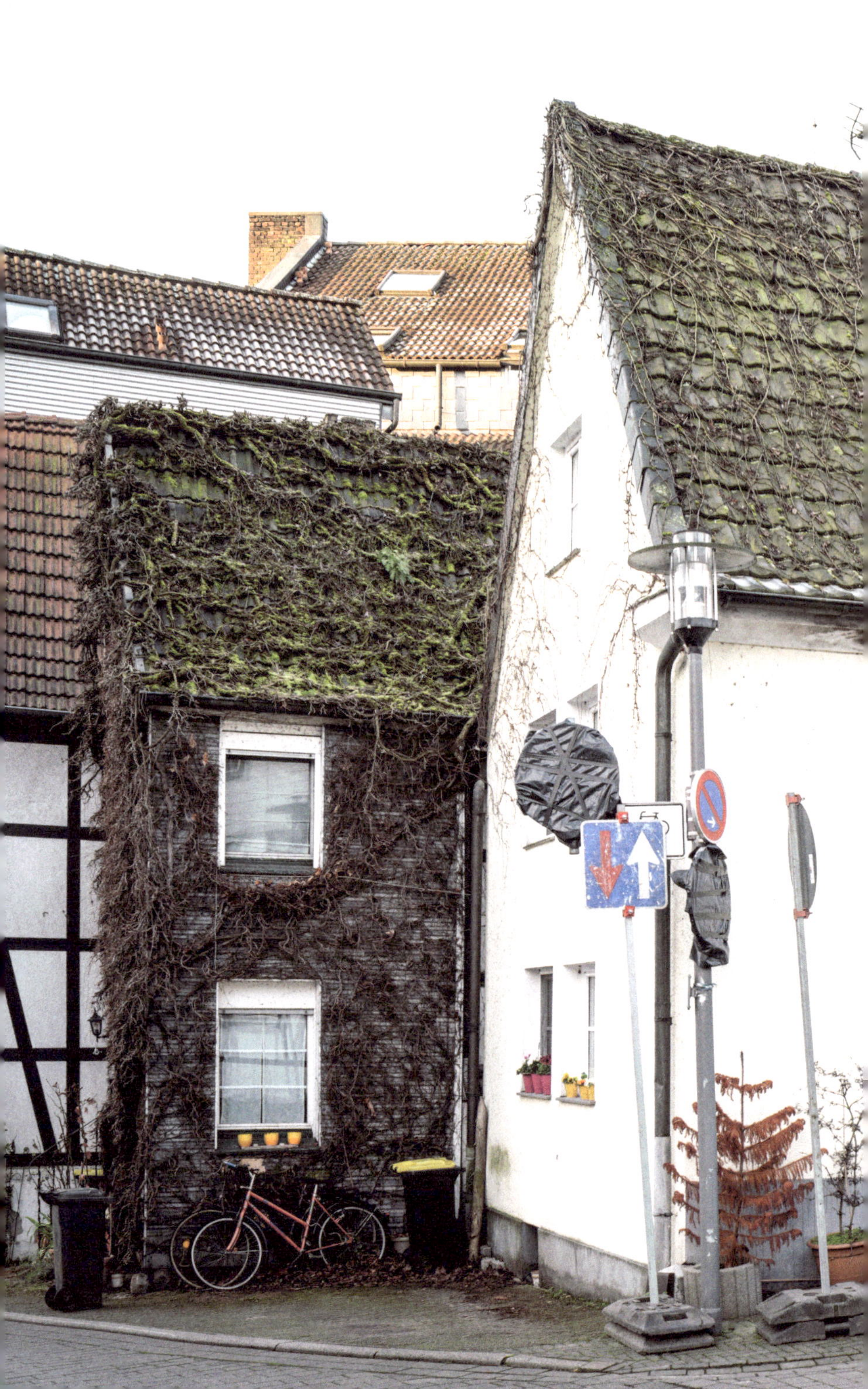

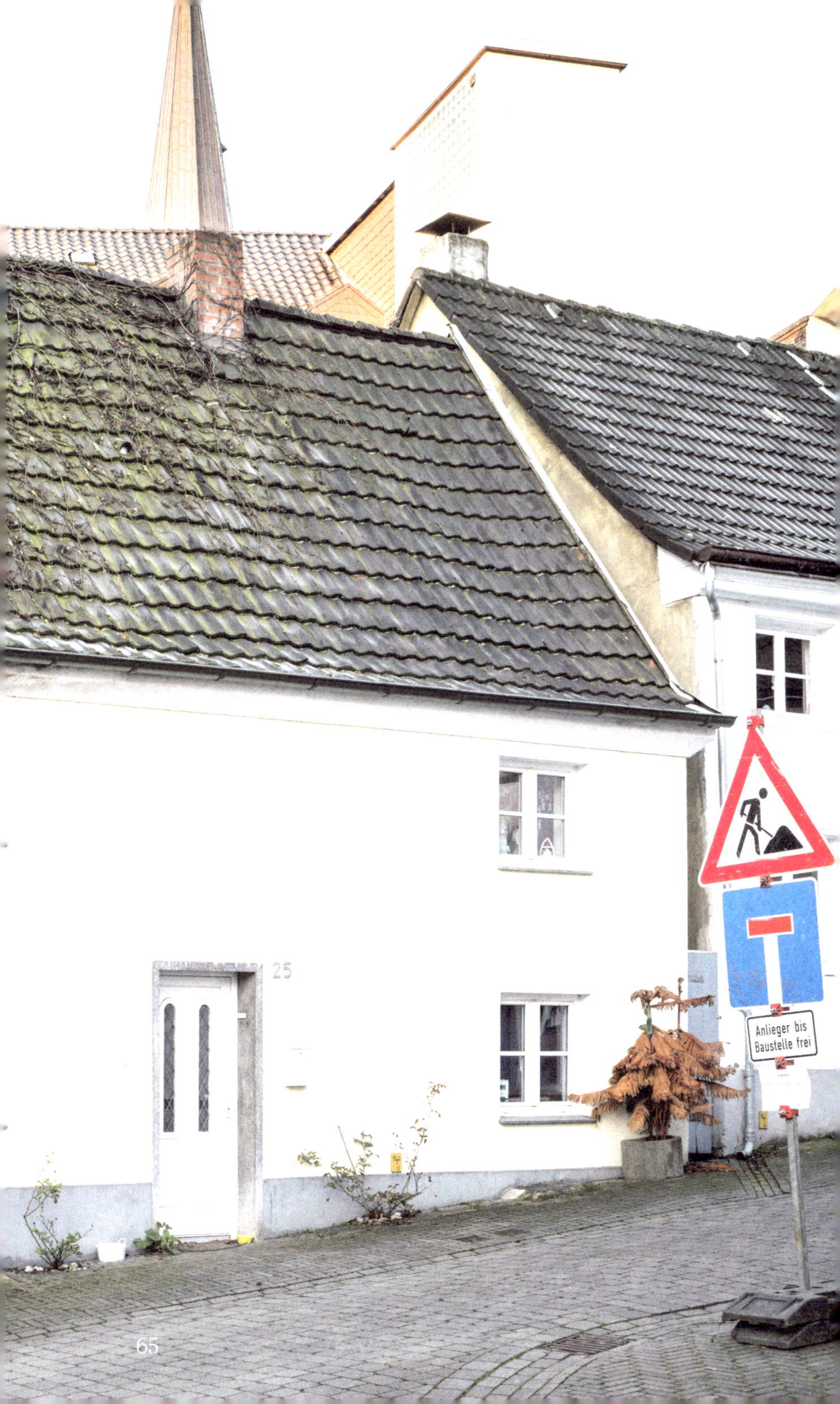
25
Anlieger bis
Baustelle frei

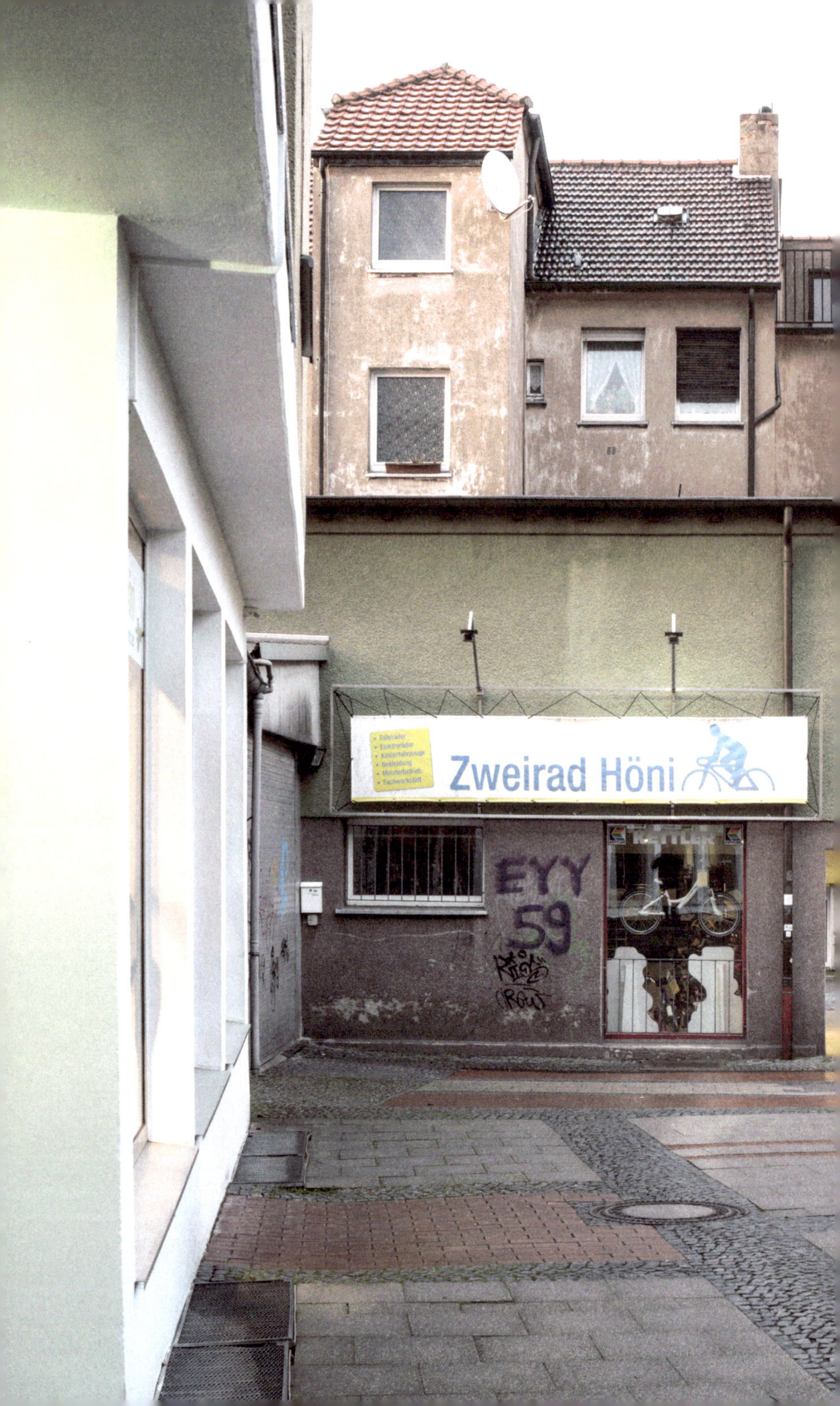
Zweirad Höni

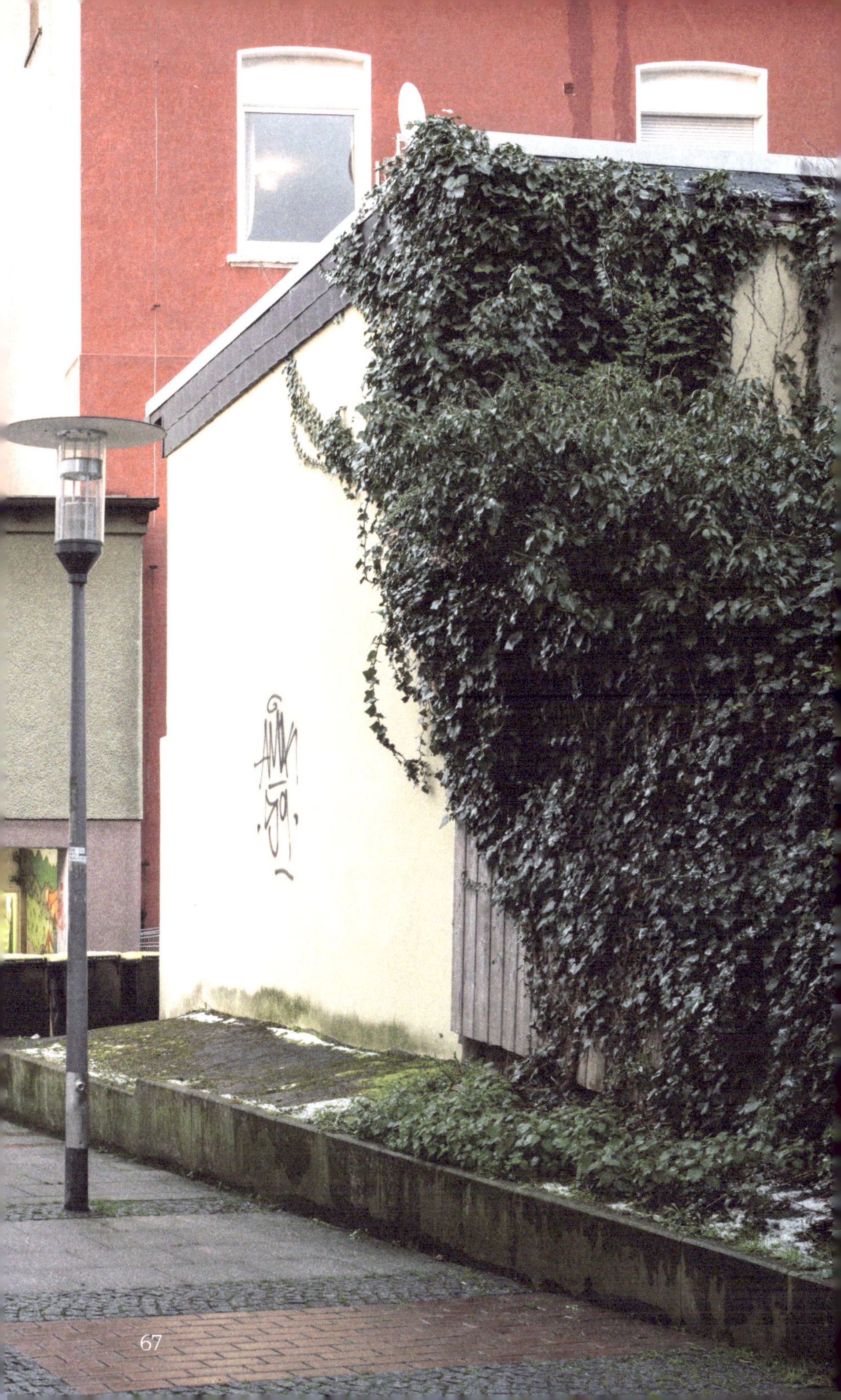

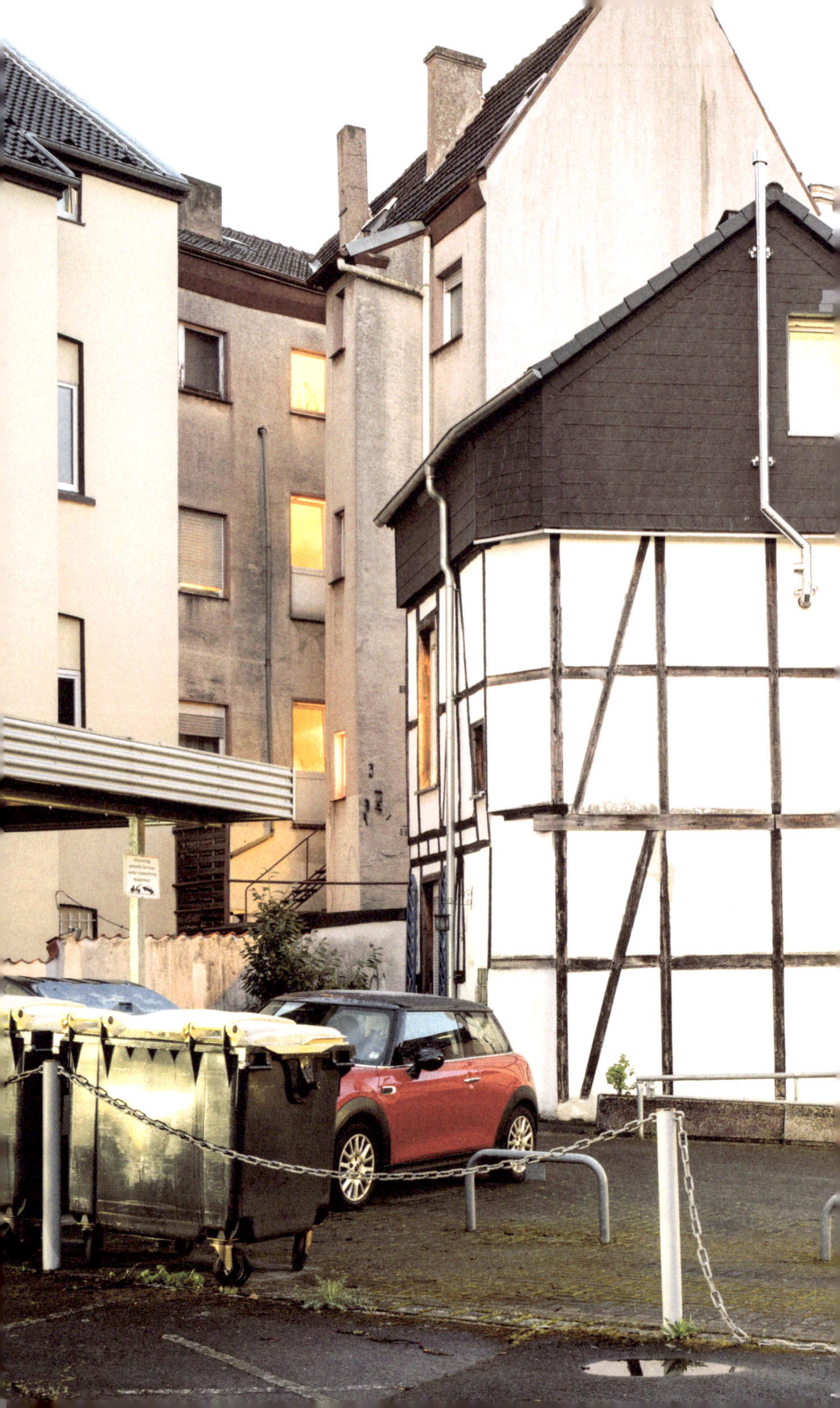

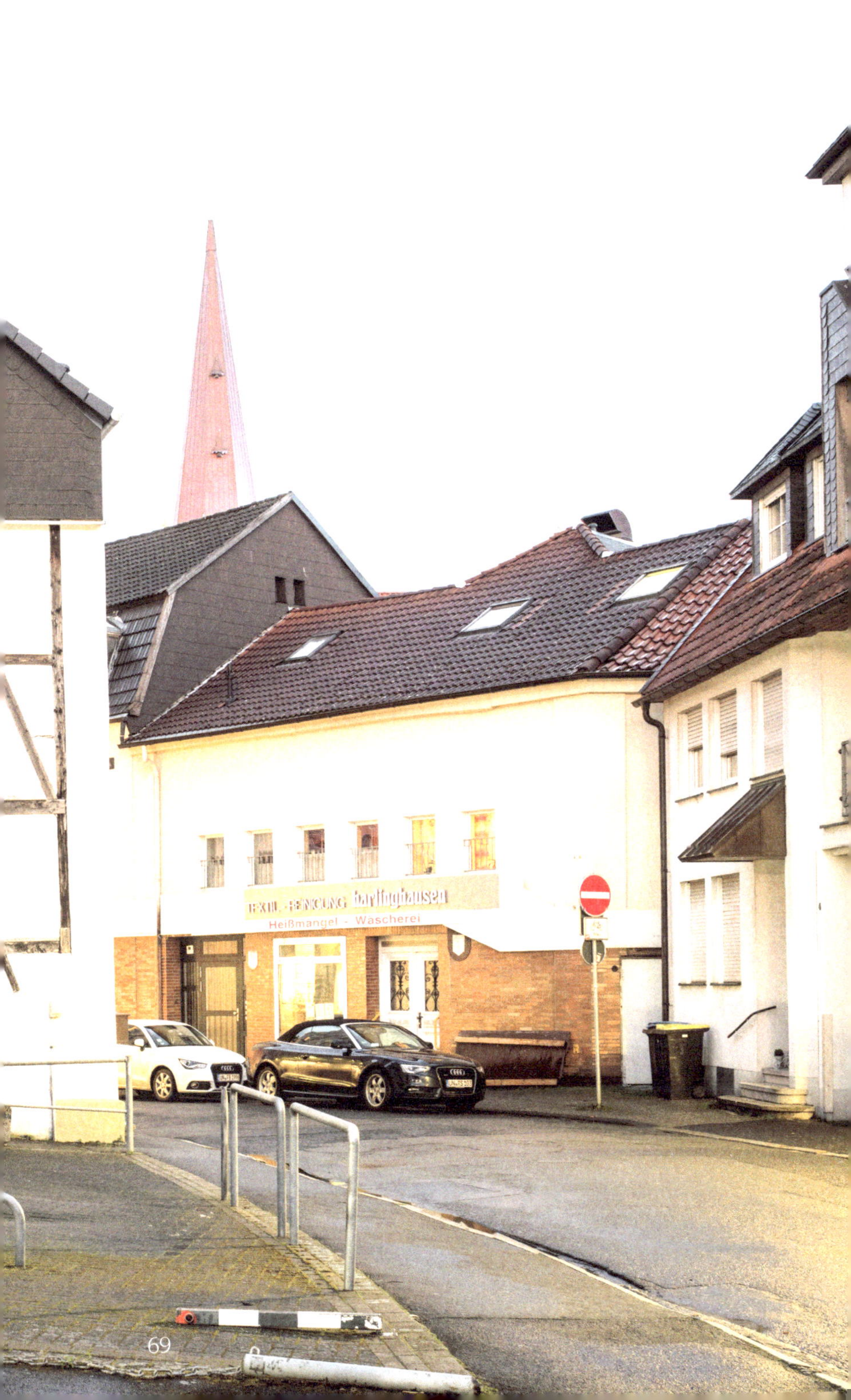
harlinghausen
Heißmangel - Wäscherei

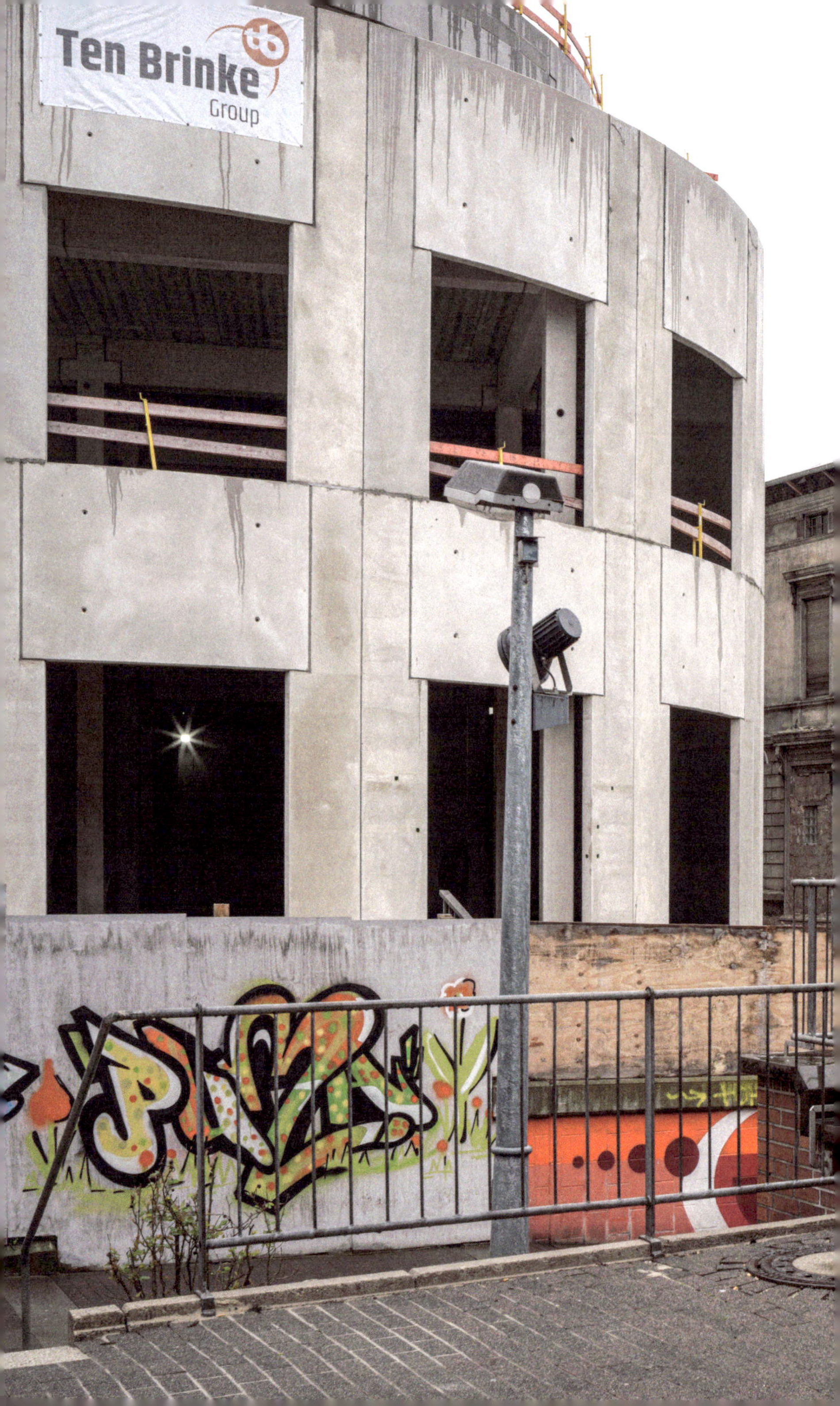
Ten Brinke
Group

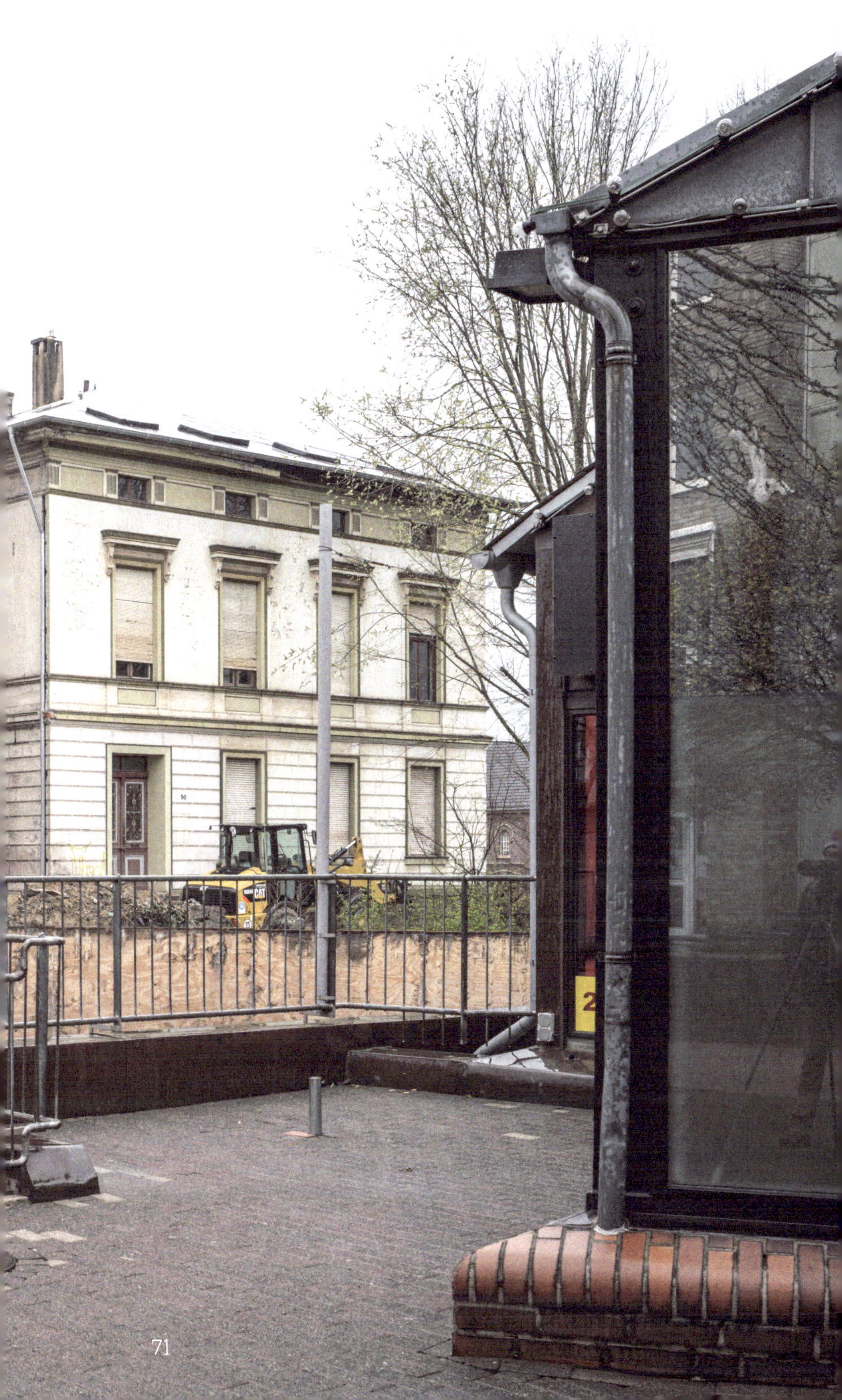

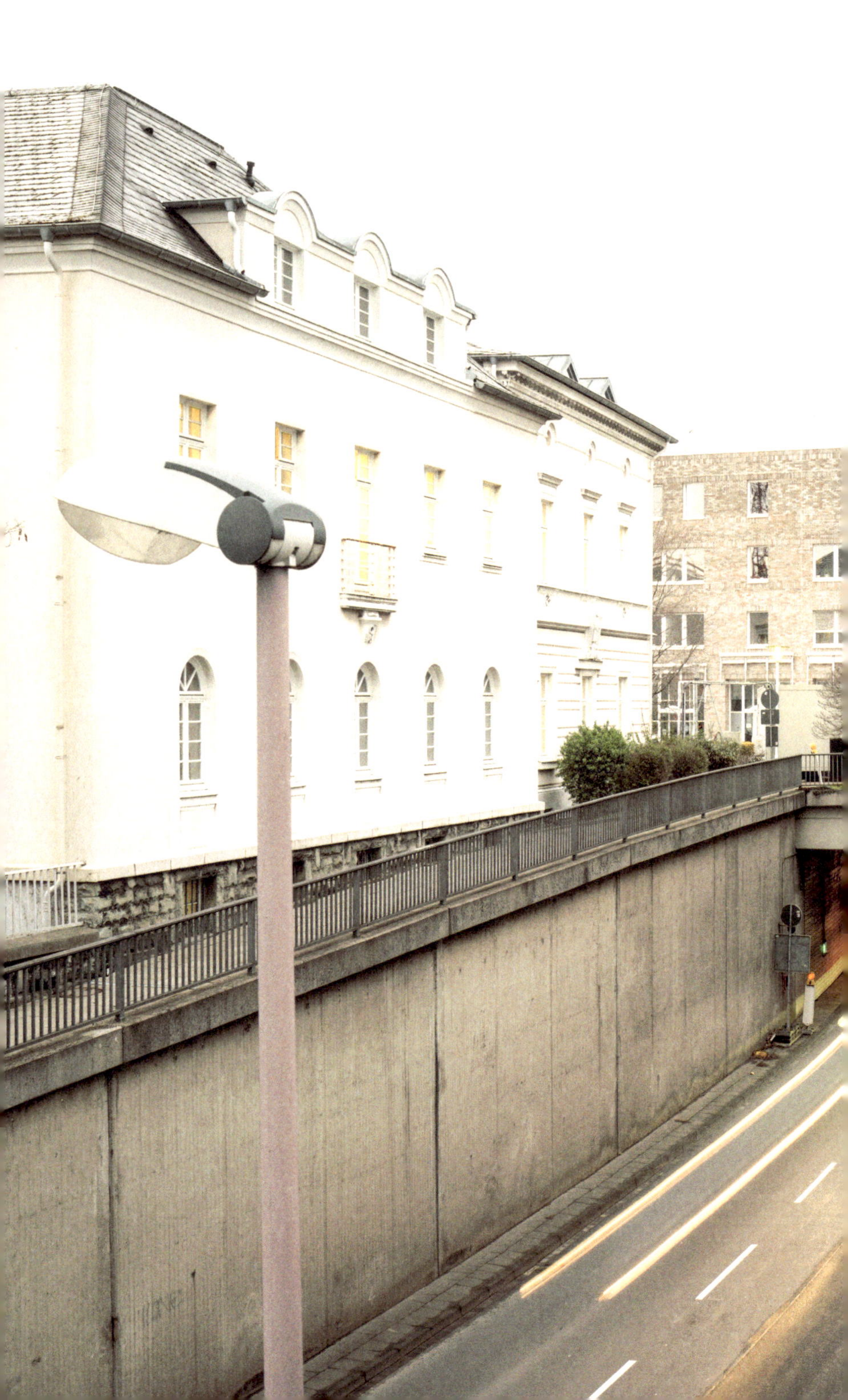

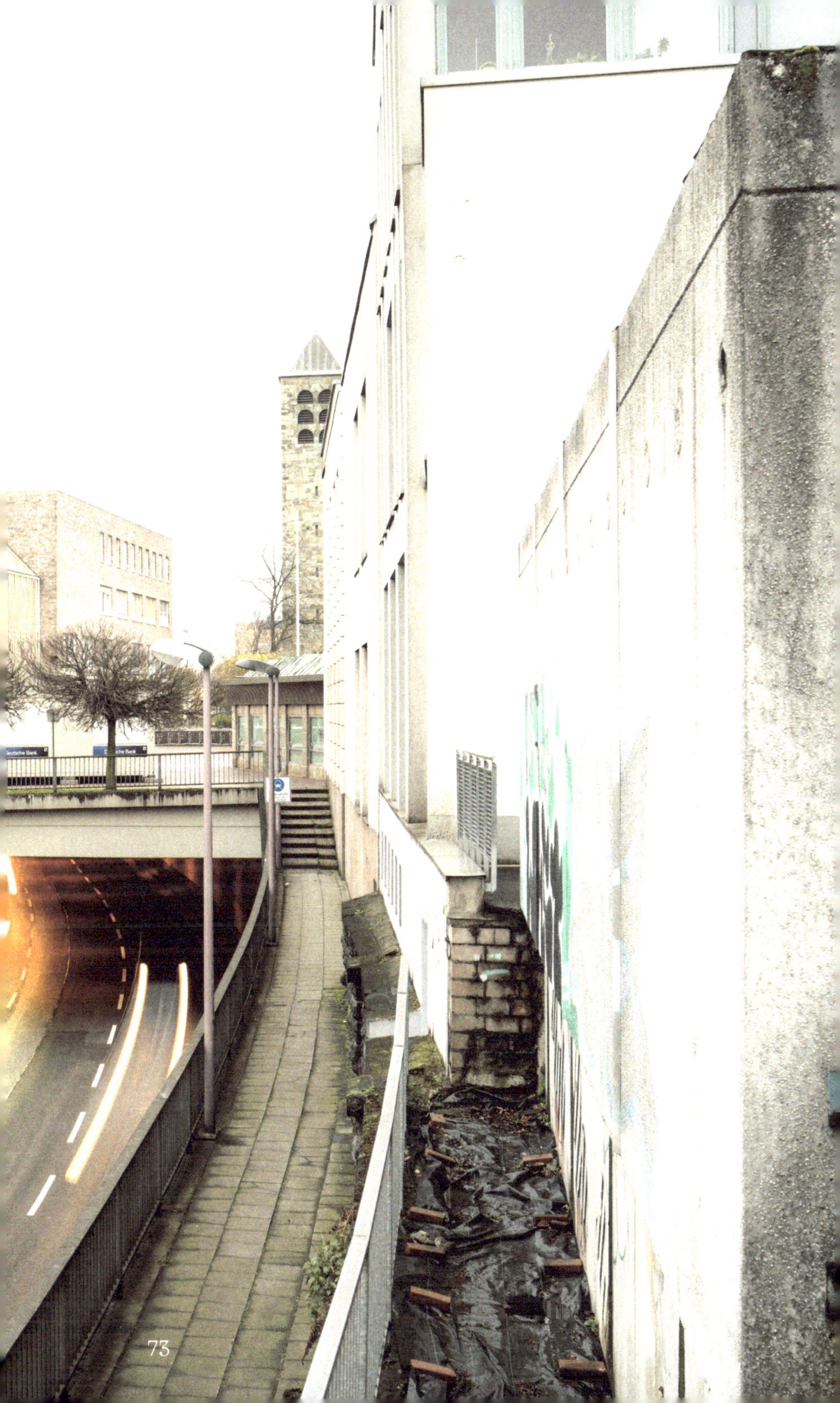
Deutsche Bank

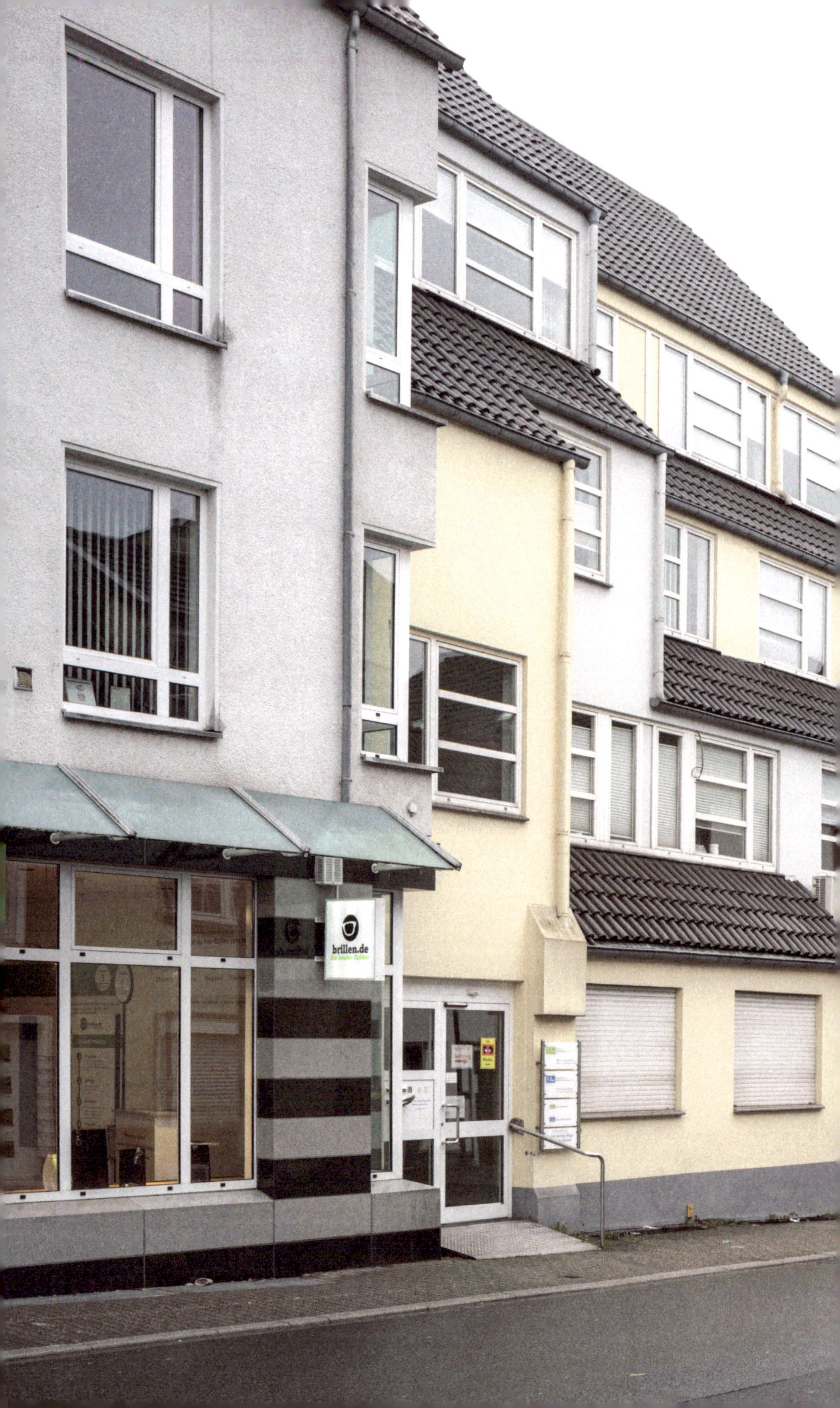
brillen.de

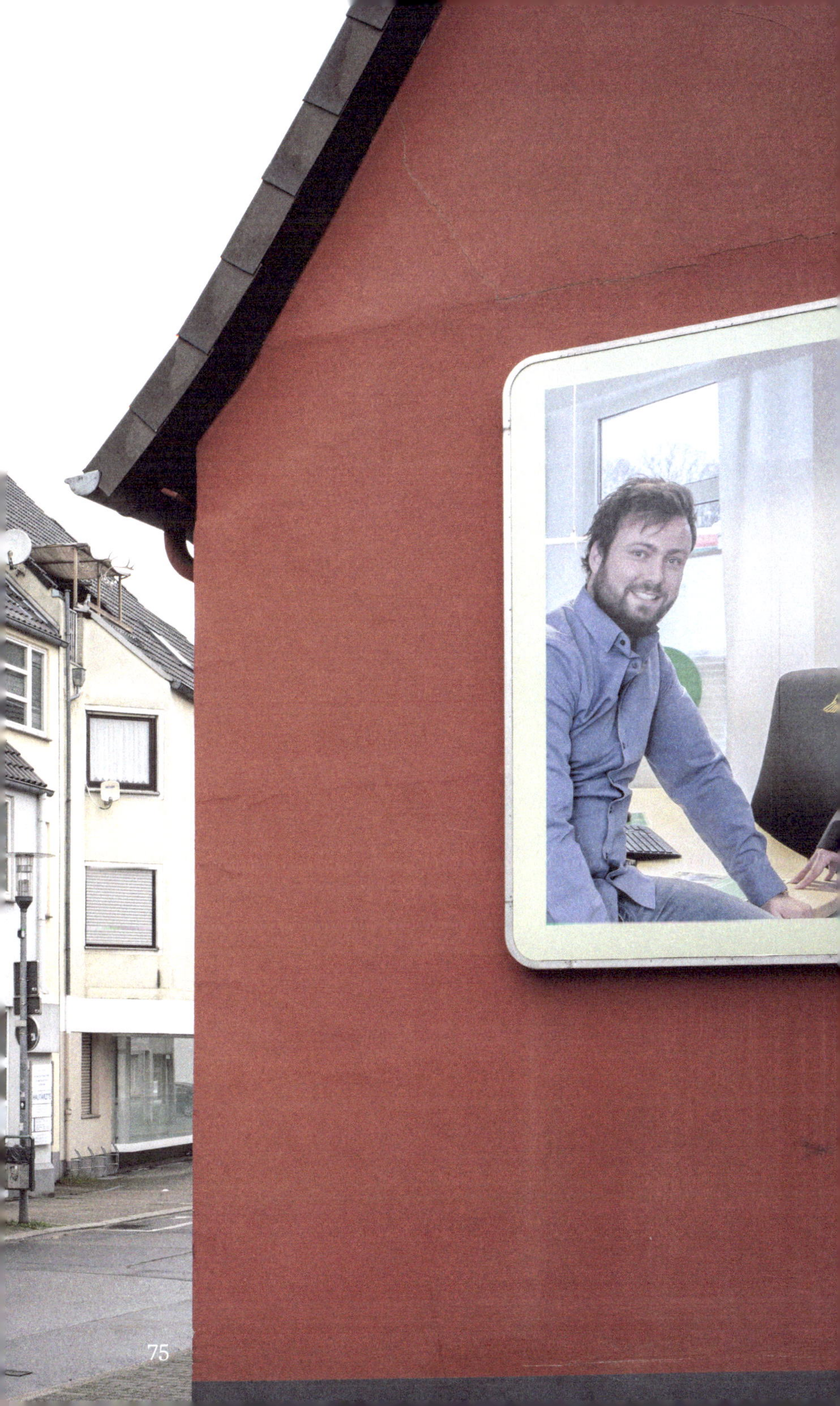

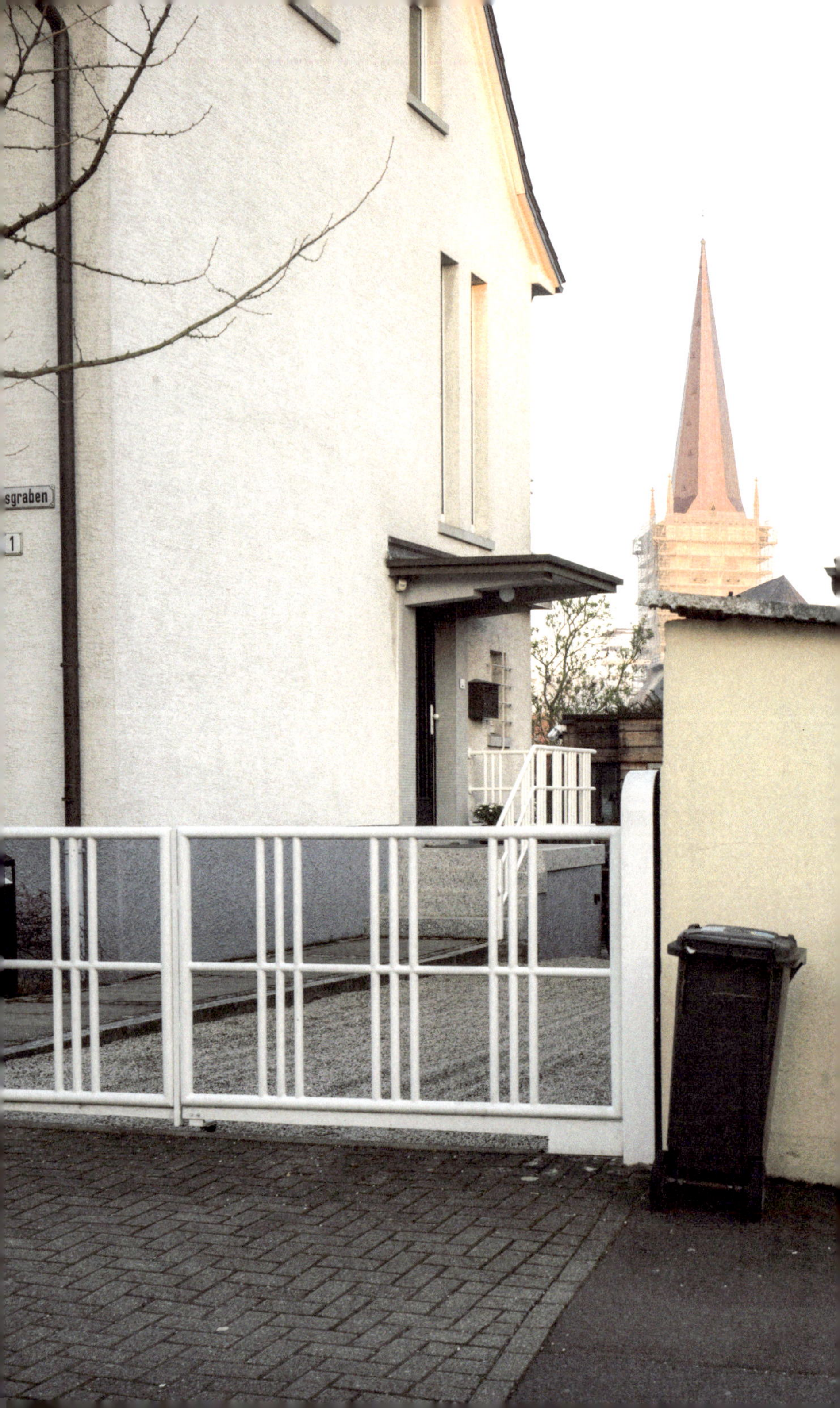
sgraben
1

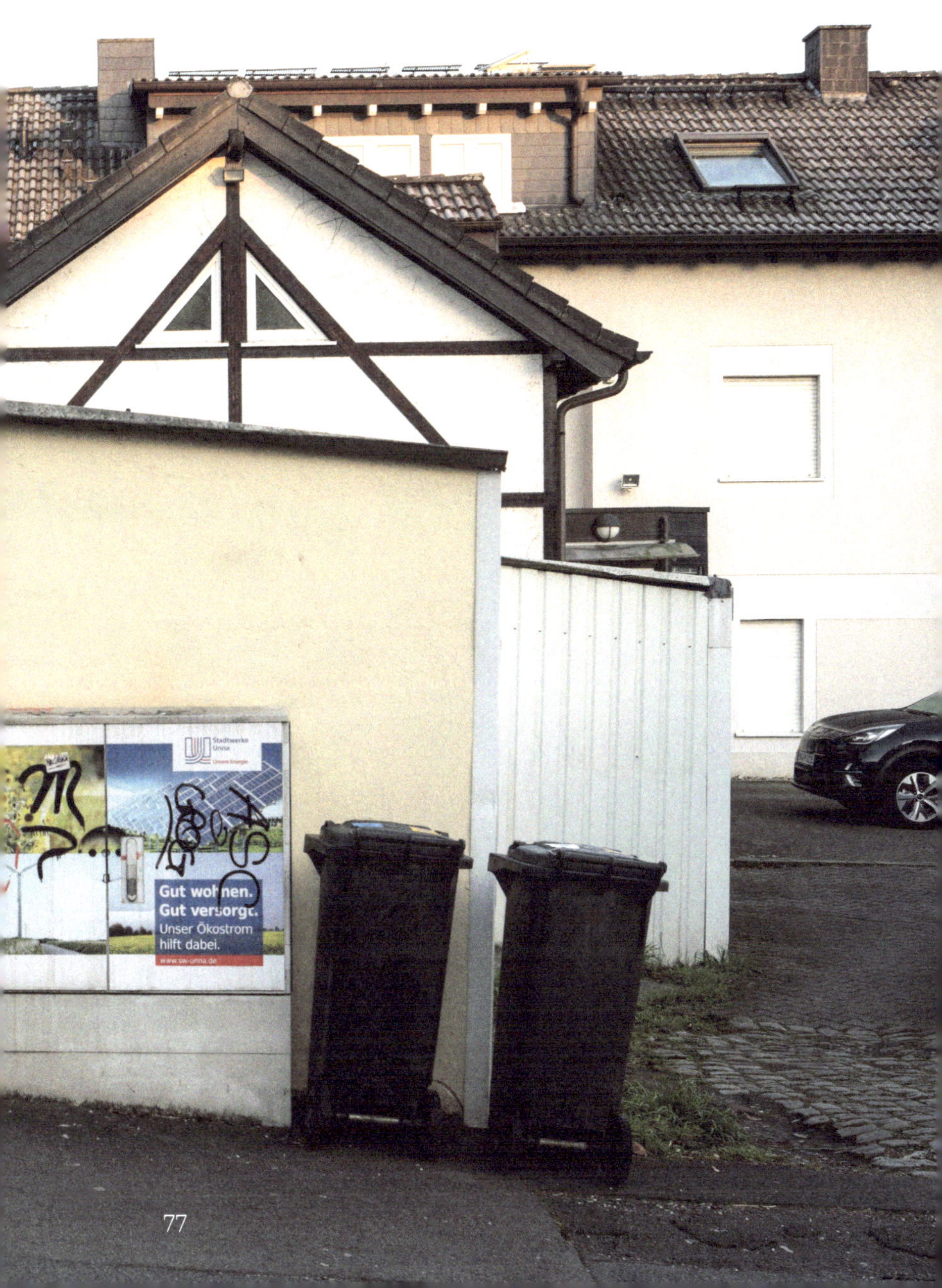

Stadtwerke
Unna
Gut wohnen.
Gut versorgt.
Unser Ökostrom
hilft dabei.
www.sw-unna.de

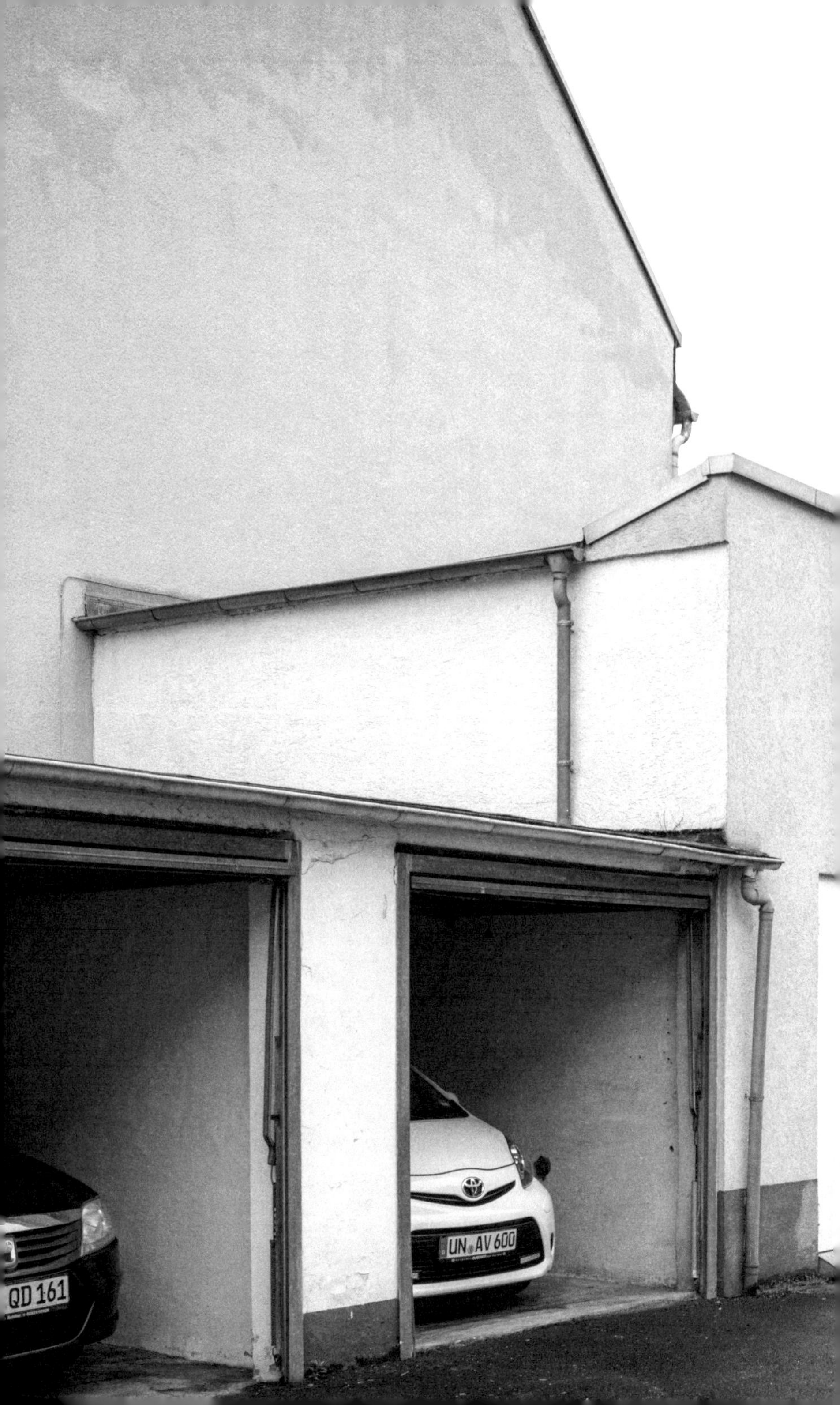
QD 161
UN AV 600

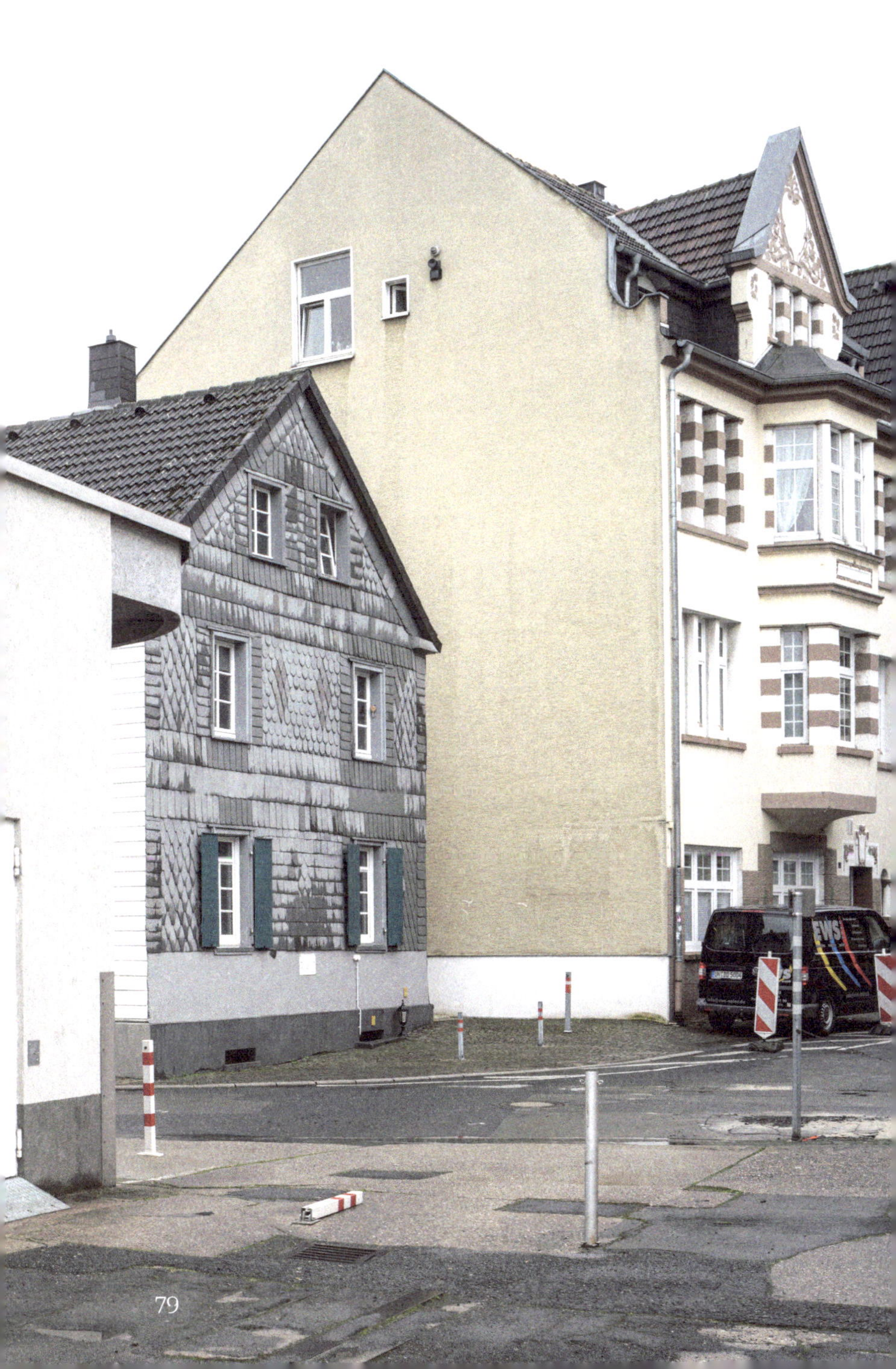
EWS

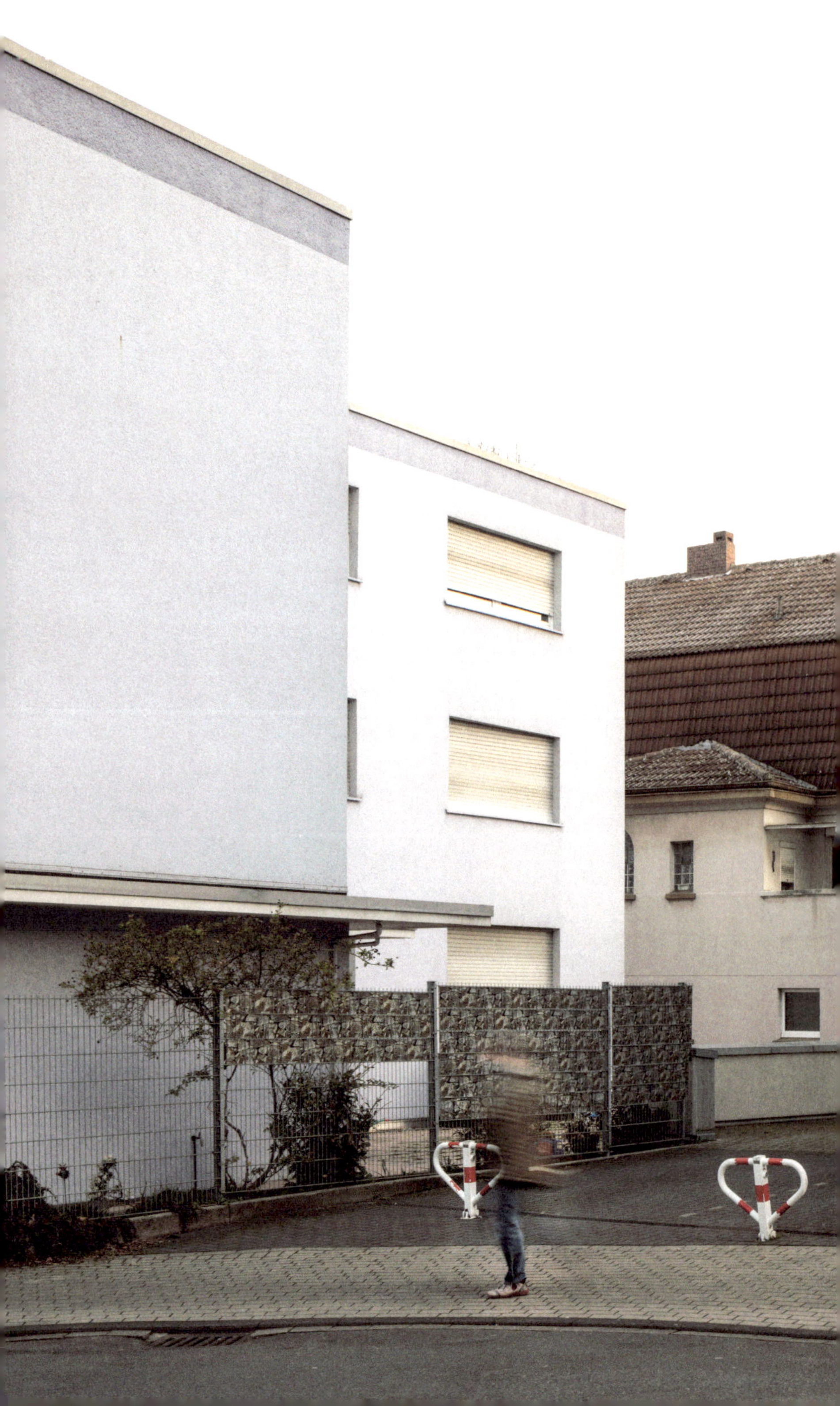

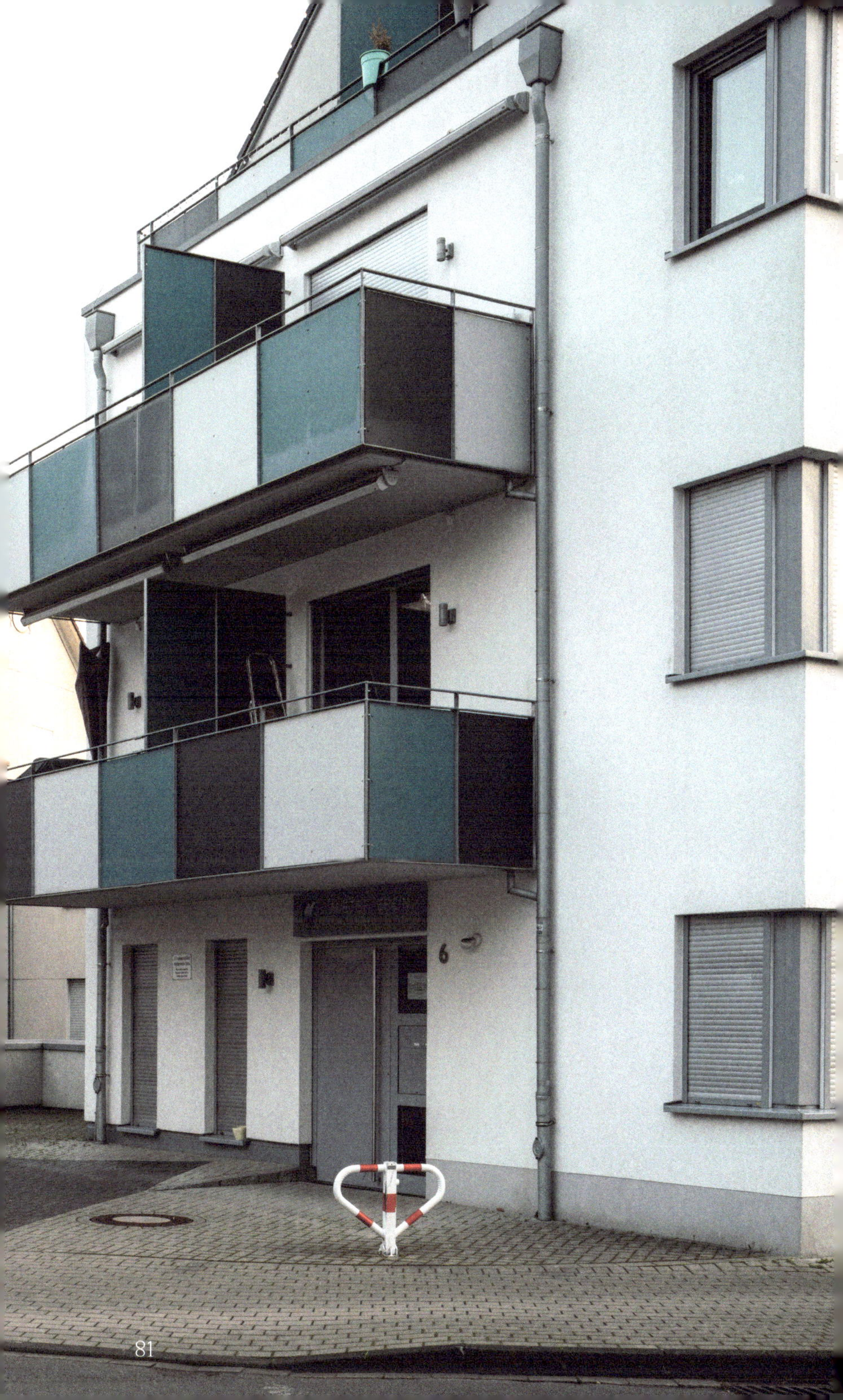
6

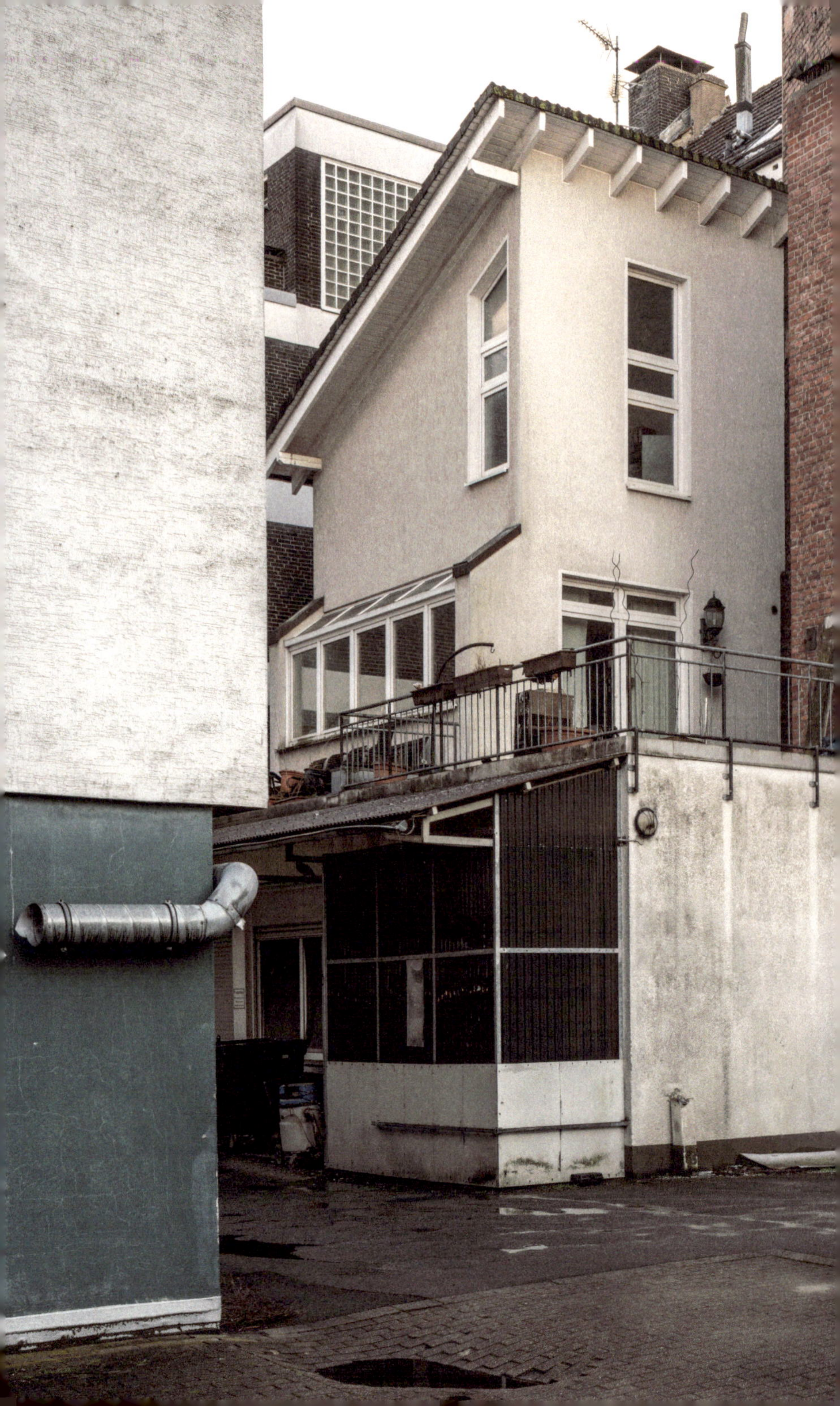

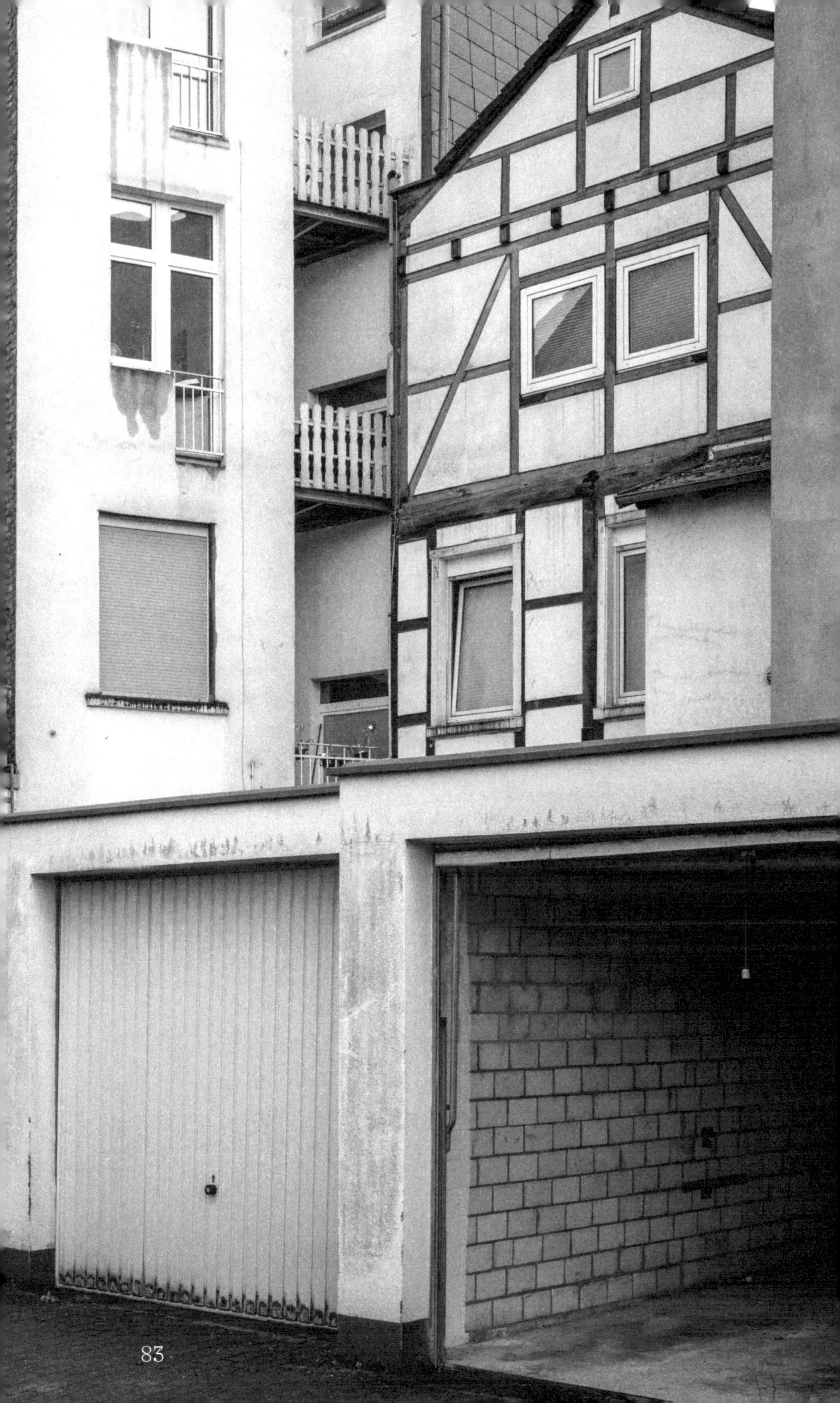

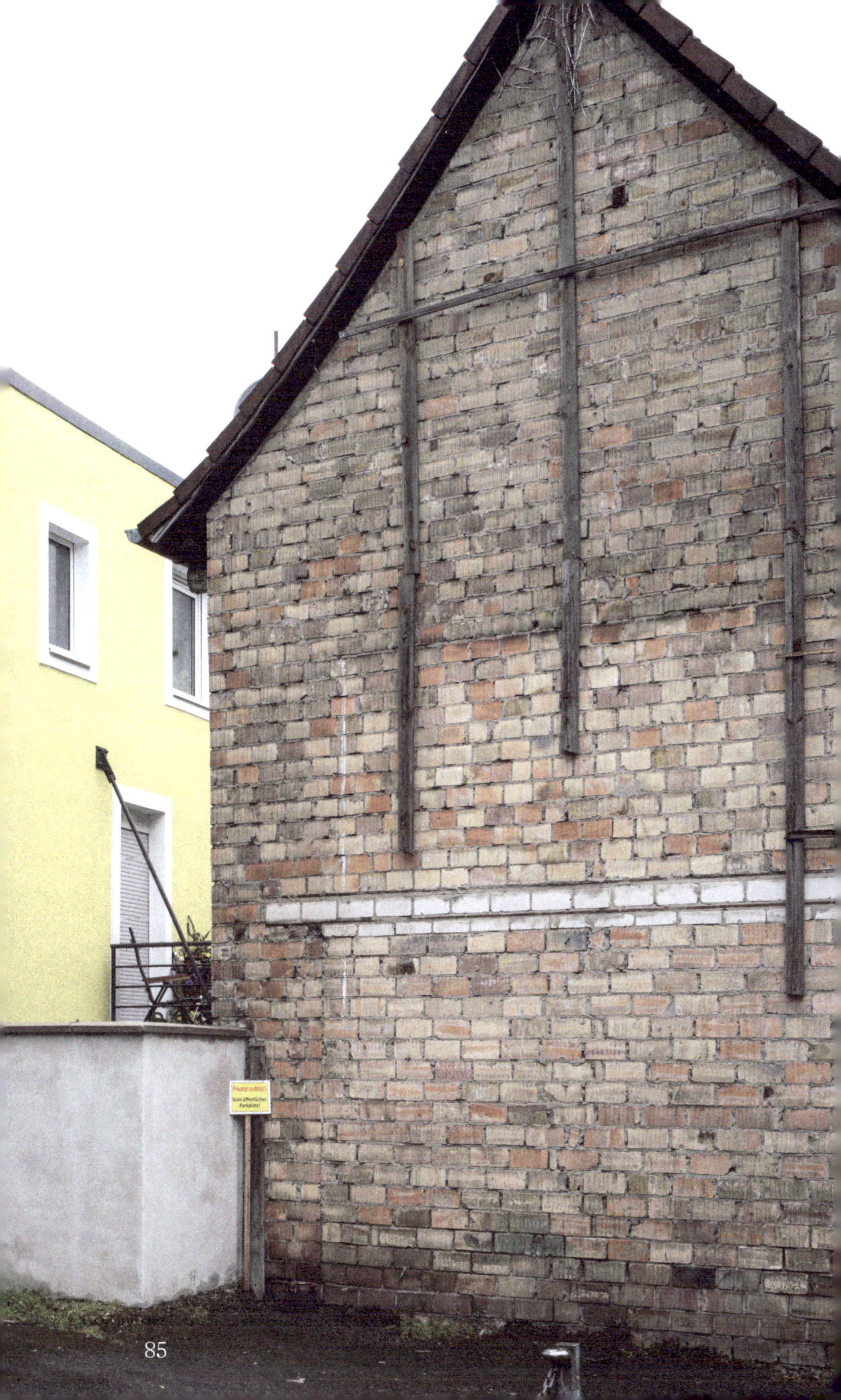
Privatgrundstück
Kein öffentlicher Parkplatz!

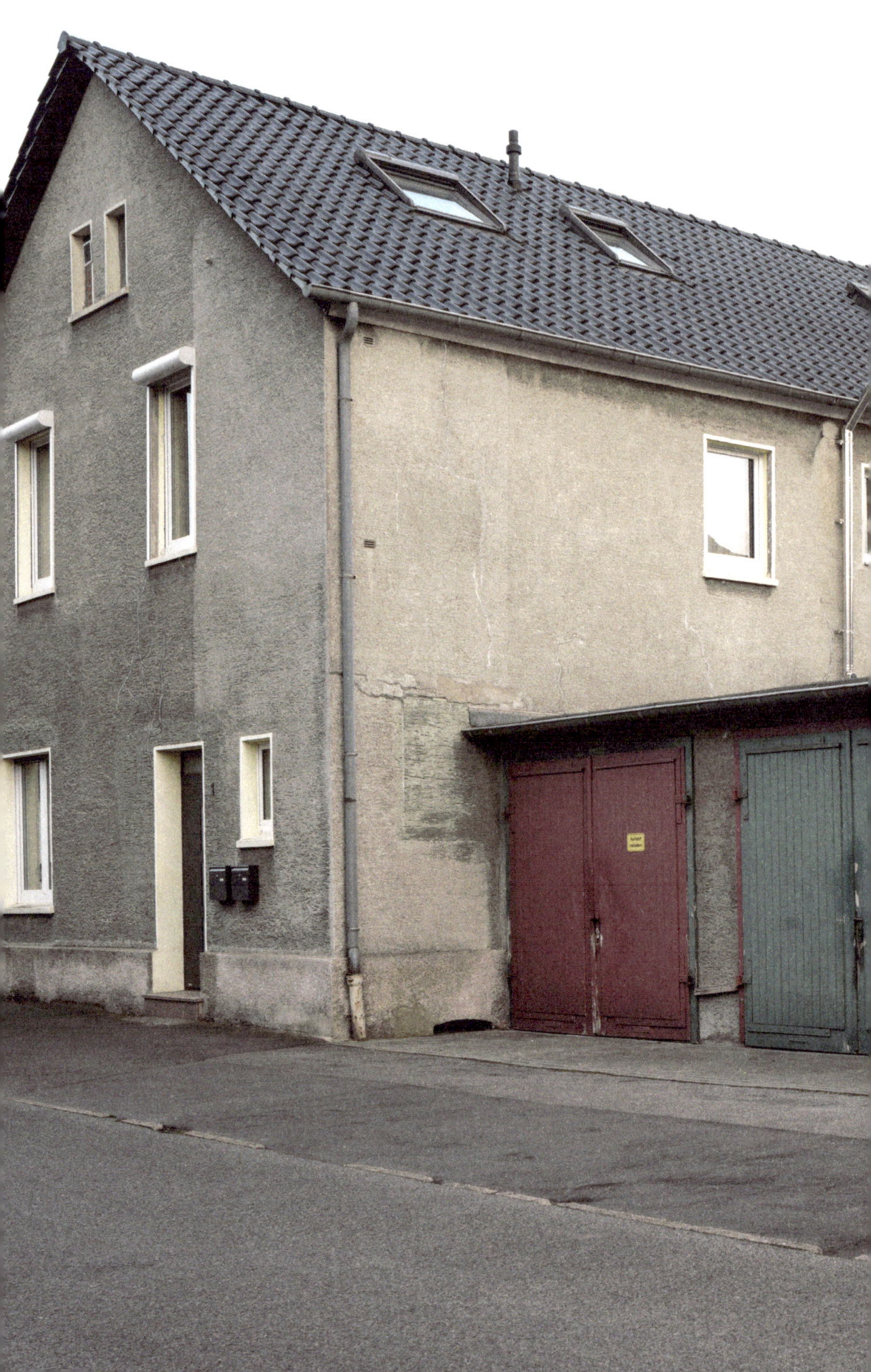

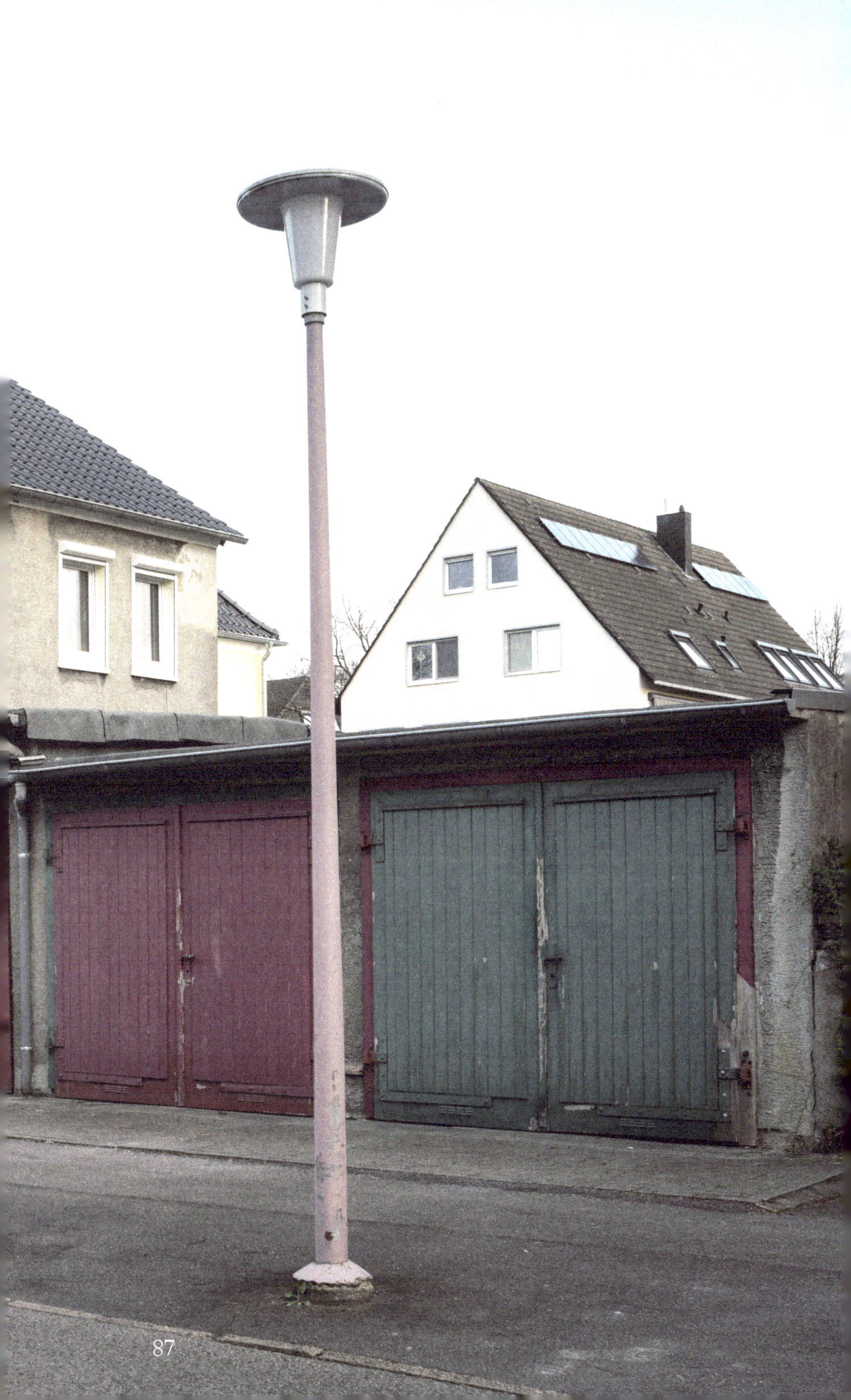

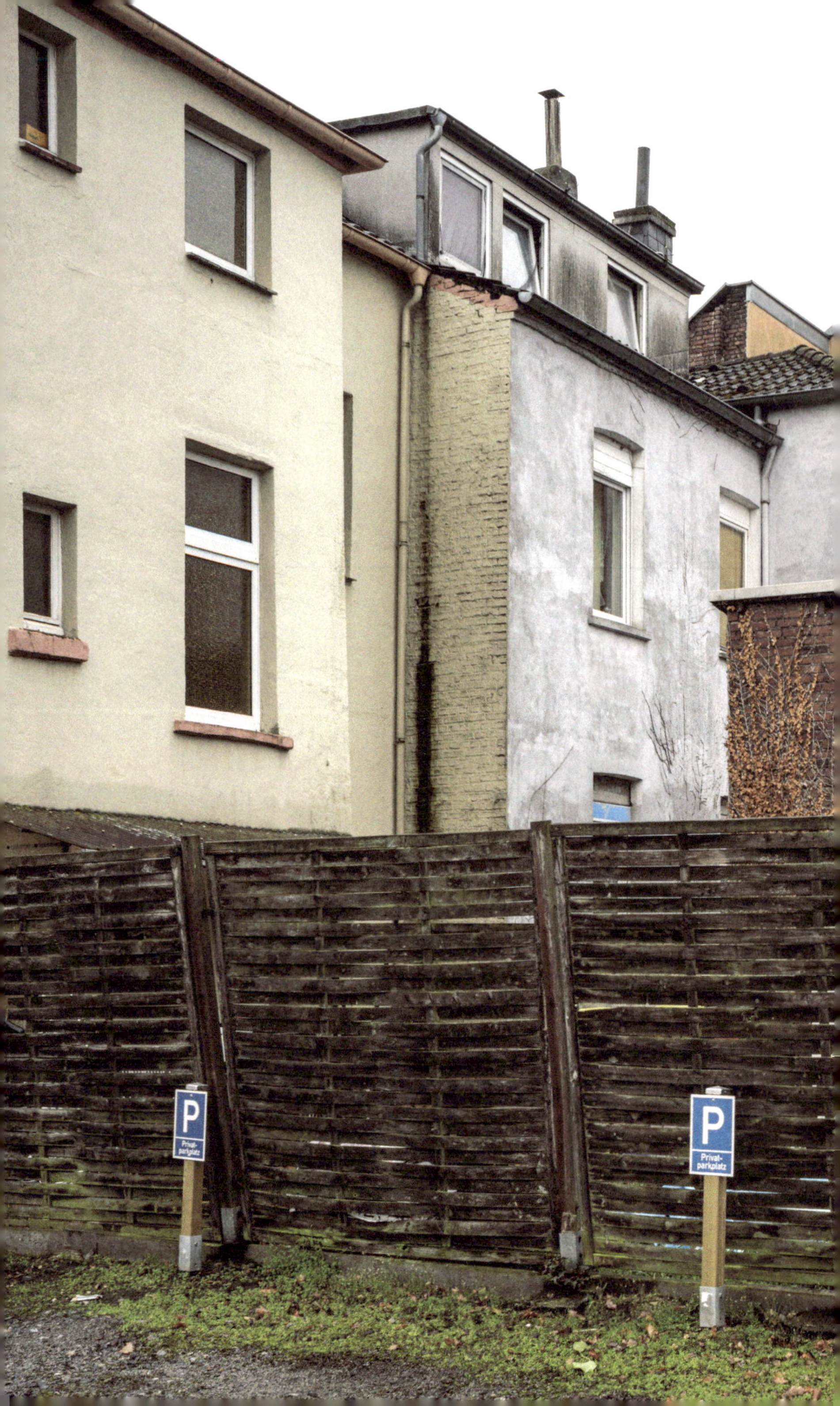
P
Privat-
parkplatz
P
Privat-
parkplatz

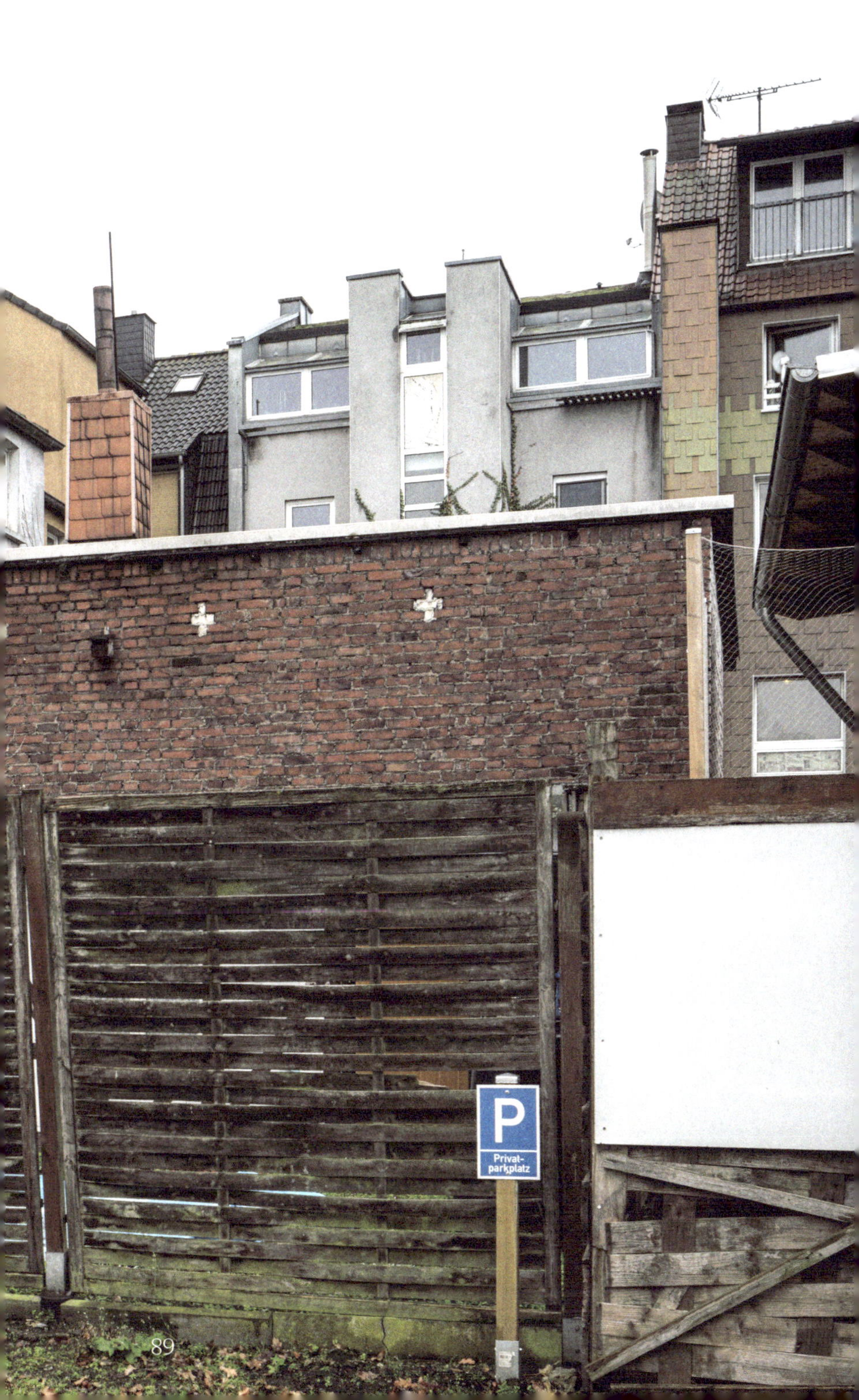
P
Privat-
parkplatz

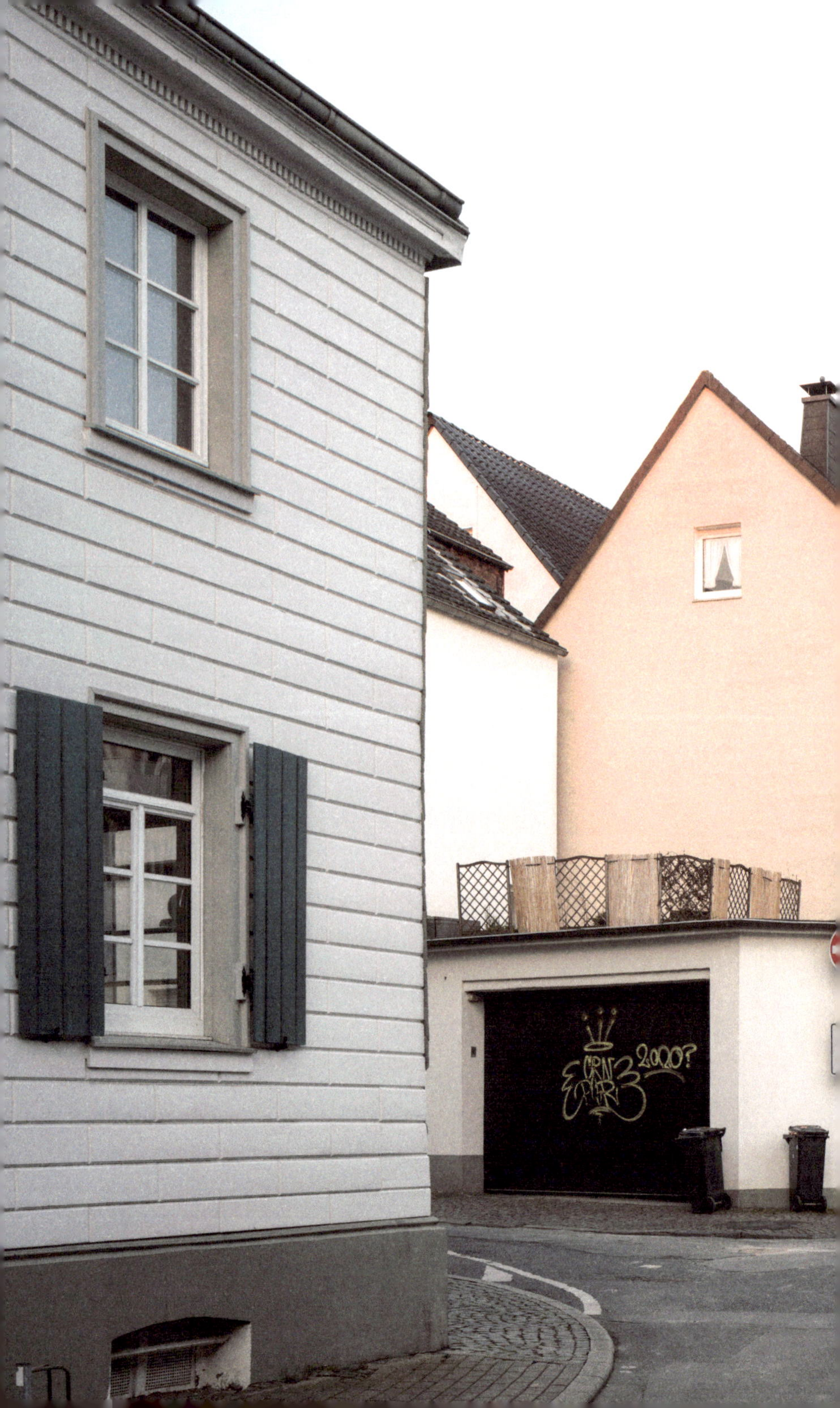
2020?

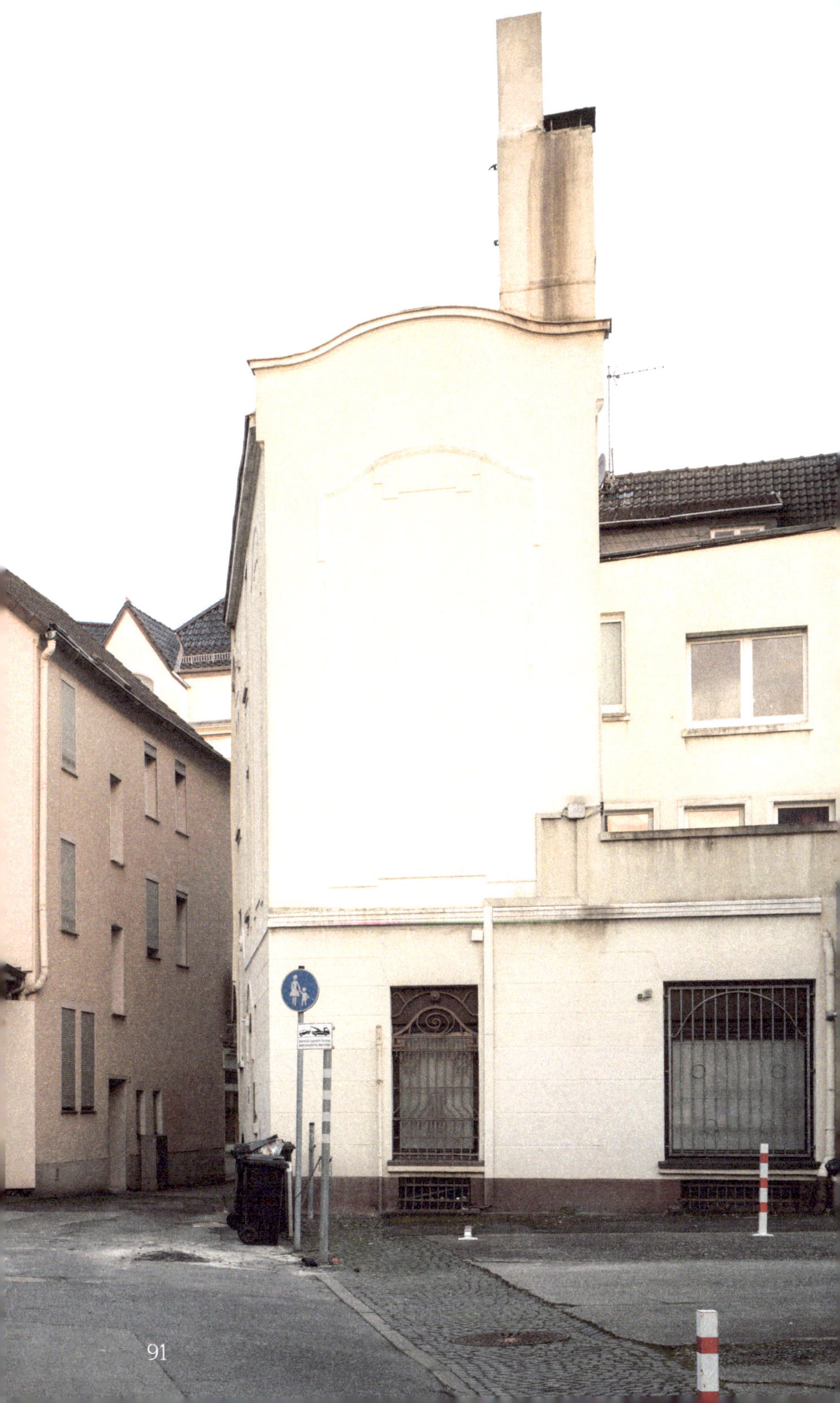

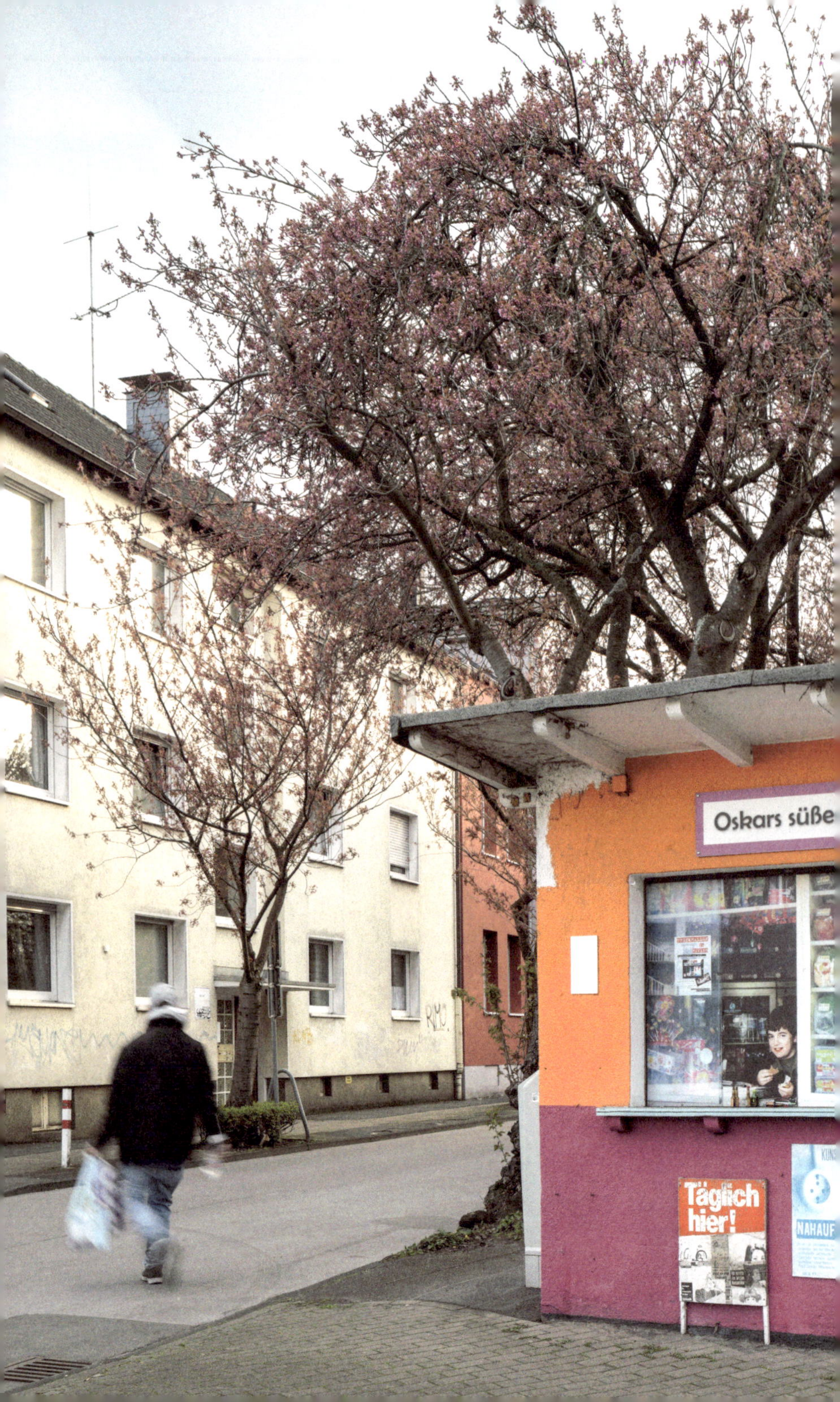
Oskars süße
Täglich
hier!
NAHAUF

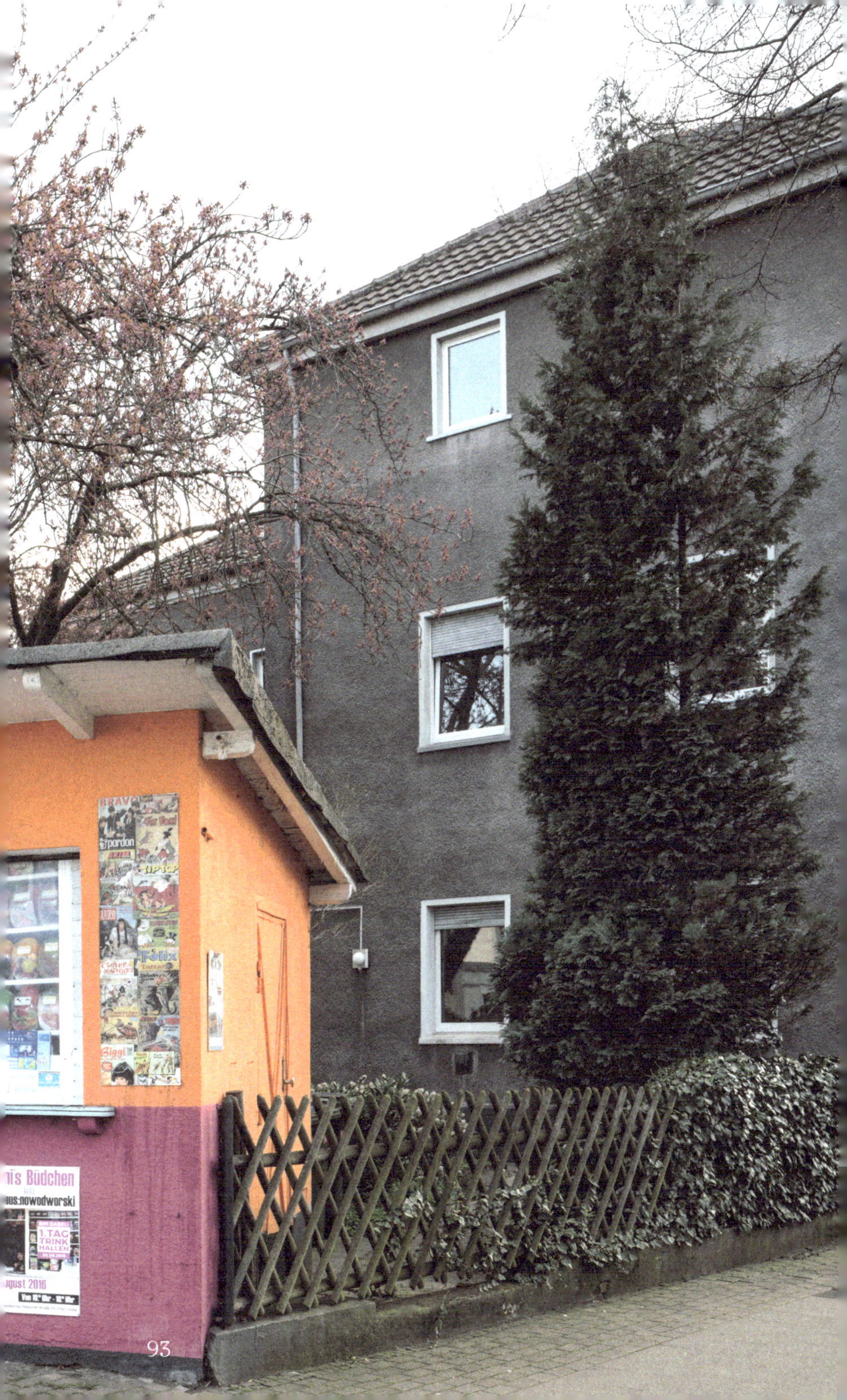
BRAVO
pardon
TIP TOP
Felix
Siggi
1.TAG
TRINK
HALLEN

Previous Diaries

Cairo Diary #1
2014
ISBN 978-1-908889-20-1

Athens Diary #2
2015
ISBN 978-1908889-29-4

Wolfsburg Diary #3
2016
ISBN 978-1908889-34-8

Taipei Diary #4
2015
ISBN 978-1908889-30-0

Kochi Diary #5
2018
ISBN 978-1908889-44-7

Beirut Diary #6
2018
ISBN 978-1908889-40-9

Wuhan Diary #7
2018
ISBN 978-1908889-64-5

Zurich Diary #8
2019
ISBN 978-1908889-65-2

Budapest Diary #9
2020
ISBN 978-1908889-66-9

Osaka Diary #10
2020
ISBN 978-1908889-56-0

Dhaka Diary #11
2021
ISBN 978-1-908889-86-7

Yangon Diary #12
2021
ISBN 978-1-908889-87-4

Minsk Diary #13
2021
ISBN 978-1-908889-88-1

Belfast Diary #14
2021
ISBN 978-1-908889-89-8

Linz Diary #15
2021
ISBN 978-1-908889-90-4

The previous diaries have been published by *thevelvetcell.com* and are available through the website.

George Town Diary #16
2022
ISBN 978-3-96070-090-6

Unna Diary #17
2022
ISBN 978-3-96070-089-0

Sarajevo Diary #18
2022
ISBN 978-3-96070-088-3

Bangkok Diary #19
2022
ISBN-978-3-96070-087-6

Available at *hartmann-books.com*

Unna Diary
Peter Bialobrzeski

Published by
Hartmann Books
Breitscheidstraße 48
70176 Stuttgart
hartmann-books.com

Photographs
Peter Bialobrzeski
bialobrzeski.net

Graphic Design and Typesetting
Sarah Fricke, Distaff Studio

Copyediting
Tas Skorupa, Berlin

Printing and Binding
DZA Druckerei zu Altenburg

Paper
Pergraphica Natural Rough

Typefaces
ABC Diatype, GT Alpina

First Edition, 2022
500 copies

ISBN
978-3-96070-089-0

This publication is kindly supported by
Kulturstiftung Sparkasse UnnaKamen

For Markus